Discovering
The Interlife

Your Journey Between Lifetimes

Discovering
The Interlife

Your Journey Between Lifetimes

Dr. Georgina Cannon

Toronto, Canada

Your work is to discover your work and then with all your heart to give yourself to it.

— Buddha

Copyright © 2008 by Georgina Cannon

Ontario Hypnosis Centre
Suite 310, 94 Cumberland Street
Toronto, Ontario M5R 1A3
Phone: (416) 489-0333 Toll Free: (866) 497-7469 Fax: (416) 484-8546
email: info@returntopastlife.com
www.returntopastlife.com

Library and Archives Canada Cataloguing in Publication

Cannon, Georgina
Discovering the interlife : your journey between lifetimes / Georgina Cannon.

Includes bibliographical references and index.
ISBN 978-0-9735311-3-8

1. Reincarnation. 2. Hypnotism--Therapeutic use. II. Title.
BL515.C28 2008   133.901'3   C2008-900732-8

Editor: Penny Hozy
Cover design: Mark Allen
Interior design: Karen Petherick Thomas

Printed in Canada

This book contains information from highly respected sources – all of which are named and cited in the Endnotes. However the author cannot assume responsibility for the validity of all materials or the consequences of their use.

CAVEAT

The author reminds the reader that the study and experience of the Interlife or Life Between Life journeys is a personal one, and can only be received as such.

Although the research by this and other authors is extensive, it does not replace the wisdom and experience of each and every personal journey taken by the reader.

The reader (not the author) assumes full responsibility for his or her experiences and journeys through the Interlife, and any subsequent emotional, physical, or intellectual responses undertaken as a result of reading this book.

This book is not intended to replace the need and requirement for any medical or other appropriate therapeutic assistance. The author does not claim that anything written in this book is the solution, in part or in whole, to any mental, physical, or spiritual problem, and should not be relied upon as such.

TABLE OF CONTENTS

ACKNOWLEDGEMENTS

First, I must acknowledge the studies and research of many before me, including Dolores Cannon, Roger Woolger, Joel Whitton, Ormond McGill, and Michael Newton, whose vocation has been the foundation and touchstone for my work with clients and students for the past years.

Secondly, my grateful thanks to the OHC graduate students who learn and relish the work of Interlife–Life Between Lives Regression Therapy. They help spread the word and healing, helping one person at a time to recognize their own magnificence. And to the clients who grace us at the clinic with their trust—my grateful, humble thanks for allowing me, and the other facilitators in the clinic, to share your soul journeys. It is an honor, and we are blessed by your presence.

Finally, to my colleagues in the clinic and the many readers of this document, including the amazing Penny Hozy and Suzanne Carlile who gave suggestions for clarity, this couldn't have happened without your support.

ABOUT THIS BOOK

With this book, I have endeavored to clarify the process of the Interlife, or Life Between Life journeying: What it is about; why do it at all; how to choose an appropriate facilitator for your personal journeying; what you can expect to get out of a journey, if and when you take one, or two; and finally, how to integrate the wisdom into your life today.

I have also included some firsthand quotes from people who have visited the Interlife, to give some idea of the type of experience you could expect for yourself. To preserve confidentiality, these cases are an amalgam of many, but they did happen, at different times and to different people. Also included is a script for a self-journey to meet your soul circle, which you may share with a trusted friend. There's also a "protection and clearing" script in the addenda to help you feel safe on the journey—a type of psychic travel insurance!

Read this book with a "believe it or not" attitude, and see if it resonates with you. See if this is the time in your life when you might want to consider taking a journey into the Interlife to find out why you are here, the purpose of this lifetime, and what you can do to make your current life richer and more fulfilling. Ultimately, this current life is the most important life—it is here and now. Do whatever you need to do to live it in peace and joy.

Introduction

You don't have a soul. You are a Soul.
You have a body.
~C. S. Lewis

It is no news to anyone that increasing numbers of people are leaving mainstream religions in droves. A widespread spiritual reawakening—a new belief system—is taking place—one that is cutting across socio-economic levels of achievement and status, and transcending cultural, political, and ethnic boundaries.

Some call it the Consciousness Age.

Your Body

During our life on this planet, 500,000 body cells die each second. Each day, about 50 billion cells in our body are replaced, resulting in a completely new body each year.

Every year about 98 percent of the molecules and atoms in our body are being replaced. Each living being is in an unstable balance of two opposing processes of continual disintegration and integration. We don't appreciate this constant change or its possible impact on our lives. But where does the continuity of our continually changing body come from? We know that cells are just the building blocks of our body, like the bricks of a house, but who is the architect; who is the engineer who coordinates the building of this house?

When someone dies, only mortal remains are left. But where is the director of the body? What about consciousness when we die? Is "someone" the body?

Do We "Have" a Body?

The belief is, at its core, that everything and everyone is part of a pattern and thus interconnected. And we connect and interconnect with each other through an altered state or transcendent state of consciousness.

Were it not a fact of experience that supreme values reside in the soul, psychology would not interest me in the least, for the soul would then be nothing but a miserable vapor.
~Carl Jung

This state allows us to "plug into" the earth and universal energies to heal ourselves and others, both directly and across boundaries. This state also allows us to access our "guides," or spirit helpers, to heal or balance our energy aura or chakras.

The medium—or energy—of this state can be achieved through hypnosis, meditation, or prayer. Many who follow the traditional religions of Christianity, Judaism, or Islam also believe "beyond the book." They believe in a state we call energy, "the light," "the Christ consciousness," "chi," or "the force."

The idea of Past Life Regression journeys isn't the shocker it once was. More and more people are recognizing that there is something beyond who we are today, right here, on this planet. And that we are truly the sum of our parts.

And whether the sum of our parts is soul parts or DNA parts, we are more than either, or both, of those.

So, like all curious travelers who wish to explore new, uncharted territory, the voyage of the soul into the Interlife can bring surprise, wisdom, occasional discomfort, awe and delight. Unlike earthly travel, you are unlikely to get tummy troubles on the journey, but then, you don't get air miles, either!

The years pass through
Like the rings of spiral,
Circle, again a circle.

Forgetting lessons learned,
Repeating previous mistakes
We all go through
Circle, again a circle.

Each spiral has its centre,
Beautiful and constant,
There lies your soul, your god, your love.
Let your centre shine
And light the next circle.

Irena Khorolsky, 2008
(translated from Russian)

CHAPTER 1

What *Is* the Interlife?

Behind me dips eternity
Before me—immortality
Myself—the term between.
~Emily Dickinson

Is It Real?

In the many years during which I have regressed thousands of people, both into past lives and the Interlife, or Life Between Lives, I have always been challenged with the question: How do I know what I experienced is real?

At the risk of sounding like a Jesuit scholar or a Kabbalist, I answer the question with another question: What do you mean by real?

Does your definition of "real" mean things you do every day? Or things and events you've heard about from somewhere or someone else?

What I can tell you, for real, is that as you learn to experience and understand more and more about death and re-birth, the exploration of the Interlife, you connect more strongly and more profoundly with your current lifetime.

Why is that? Exploration allows growth and understanding—for the same reason that the more you travel to other countries, the more you interact with other cultures, the more you embrace your own. We bring the eagle-eye view to everything we encounter—whether we encounter it physically, emotionally or spiritually.

And truly, the eagle-eye view is what you get when you journey through the Interlife—or Life Between Lives of your soul journey.

So what *is* the Interlife, or Life Between Lives?

If you believe in reincarnation in nature—like the seed of a plant recycling through the seasons—then you believe also that it is so with us, that the seed of who you are leaves one body and returns in another. And if you don't believe in reincarnation, then allow the journey to be considered as a metaphor created by your mind to bring healing and understanding. Are you OK with that?

Think of it as one door opening and another closing—but what about the corridor between the doors? What about the time between these incarnated lifetimes?

We enter a place that the *Tibetan Book of the Dead* calls Bardo, or the Interlife, or the Labyrinth, or the Blue Mist of Life Between Lives.

Joel Whitton describes this as "metaconsciousness," a state of memory awareness in which we merge into existence itself, causing us to lose all sense of personal identity, while at the same time becoming more intensely self-aware than ever. He explains that ...

> ... while this might suggest an atmosphere of free-floating, cottonwool emptiness, the life between life is not a fairy-tale world. Those who have tasted its richness know that they have visited the ultimate reality, the plane of consciousness from which we embark on successive trials of incarnation and to which we return at the death of the body.[1]

Within this space, this place, is a journey of discovery, where you might meet your soul circle, discover your immortal name, your soul color. You might journey to a laboratory or school for more learning. You might go to a place of rest or soul relaxation to heal and recover from a traumatic incarnation. You will probably meet your council of advisors, and go to a place to choose your next incarnation, and find out why you have to reincarnate—the purpose of your current life, and why you chose the body you currently inhabit.

Does everyone take the same journey? No. But they are remarkably similar even if the journeyperson has never discussed the concept previously, or read anything about traveling to the Interlife. According to Winafred Lucas:

> Recovery of Interlife experiences may become the spiritual thrust of the future. Like near-death experiences, they facilitate a transformation of consciousness and encourage an attitude of

compassion, but unlike NDEs, they are under consciious control. Each traveler through the Interlife can obtain exactly what is appropriate for his stage of growth.[2]

So, as in this life, we see what we believe. If you are a fundamentalist Christian, and you believe in purgatory, when you first start your Interlife Journey, you may well see fire and brimstone, and so it goes until you reach the upper levels of vibration and come into your true essence, leaving any vestige of your body / mind behind.

Those who have reported personal observations of a life between life can be compared to the mariners of old who returned from a long voyage south with an absurd tale of the sun shining from the north ... To venture into the unknown is often to savor experiences that confound contemporary wisdom.[3]

Recorded History

The recorded research around Interlife journeys is comparatively recent. But the journeying itself has been recorded for thousands of years.

Although it is believed that the early Egyptians were the first to teach the concept of the soul's being immortal, Pythagoras, the Greek philosopher, brought the concept into full fruition when he taught it as if it were his own.

Pre-Columbian civilizations, such as Aztecs, Mayans and Toltecs (2000 BCE–14th Century), believed in the Interlife. Egyptian mythology

(2500 BCE) also strongly considered the Interlife as part of existing life and religion—hence the packing of pets, wives, mistresses and other worldly goods into tombs along with the interred bodies. Currently, and since they began hundreds of years before the time of Christ, both the Hindu and Buddhist religions also believe in the Interlife or Bardo.

> *In the between-life state the soul reviews its performance across many lifetimes and chooses to resolve or atone for certain deeds in the next life. While past mistakes confront the soul in the bardo, most karmic adjustments can only be made by returning to physical existence and reencountering, in many instances, those with whom the karma has been established.*[4]

The Interlife, the space or corridor between incarnations, is the time we are given to consider our karmic destiny and make the choices that will best fulfill that destiny. The Tibetans have always been aware of this and still hold sacred *The Tibetan Book of the Dead*, written by the great master Padma Sambhava in the eighth or ninth century, as a guide to the journey between lifetimes.

The Tibetan description of the "Interlife" differs in many ways from the contemporary version of Life Between Lives. For instance, it doesn't contain a Council for the life review. Nor does the more ancient version include the element of conscious learning. We are, in the modern day, more conscious of the ability to make specific choices around the journey of our lives.

For centuries, Aboriginal shamanistic journeys often passed through a form of Interlife as they made their way through the passages of soul lifetimes, taking on the form of plants or animals to gather wisdom from a different point of view, and sometimes completely physically shape-shifting while on the journey.

In all cases the Interlife is seen as a place of peace and rest as well as a place of learning before the soul evolves into a different state of consciousness or a higher realm

The Goal of the Interlife

> I see the potential for a new world being born in front of me and all around me, and I feel the only way to bring that potential into being is to know myself.
> ~Gary Zukav

During our time in the Interlife, we learn that the ultimate goal on the physical plane—the here and now—is to know ourselves. During our lifetime, we are offered many lessons—some of which are painful—but all will challenge us to know who we are.

However, we also learn that our experiences are given to us by ourselves. We choose what is to be experienced in the life, so that we can learn the lessons we need to learn.

Our journey through the Interlife, or Life Between Lives, is a time for reflection and learning. We are here to make important decisions, and the more we understand about our life lessons, the better prepared we will be to learn from them and to know who we really are.

Your ultimate power lies in the fact that you can leave any situation that is not to your liking. You can leave for a few minutes, you can leave for a few hours, or you can leave for good. This means that you never have to be a victim again.[5]

Soul Levels—As we understand them

Both the *Tibetan Book of the Dead* and the *Egyptian Book of the Dead* suggest that immediately after death everyone is able to perceive the Clear Light. However, some souls may be drawn because of anger, desire or misused lifetimes to less luminous states. Many people seem unaware that their souls are on a journey. And maybe because of that, the periods between lifetimes are uneven in length— some souls needing a longer learning period in the life between lives, where others want or need a speedy reincarnation, as they feel their previous lifetime wasn't complete in some way or other.

The levels we attain, therefore, show us where we are currently and how far we have yet to journey. As I tell my clients: If we don't get it right in this lifetime, we'll have to come back and repeat the same lesson again!

1st level   ...The Elementals—pure energies— rocks, trees, water, the earth. Life forms with no individual personality—collective life forms waiting for their time.

2nd level   ...Elementals who deal with the plants, trees, and animals, or the land, sea, and air. Also called dryads, sprites, fairies, leprechauns, devas. They have more mischief than intelligence. They exist in the spirit realm—their souls are working toward perfection, just like ours. After they have learned to take care of nature, then they can move up and learn to take care of themselves.

3rd level	...Humans who do not have the intelligence to be either good or bad; they just live an existence. Animal group souls are also at the 3rd level.
4th level	...Humans who are antisocial, criminals, and murderers.
5th level	...Humans on earth level of day-to-day existence.
6th level	...The spirit realm—also some humans who are open and aware.
7th level	...The soul schools—where we go in the Interlife.
8th / 9th levels	...The Great Masters—Avatars, Jesus, Buddha.
10th level	...One again with God.

CHAPTER 2

What Is This State We Call Death?

Death is not extinguishing the light;
it is putting out the lamp because the
dawn has come.
~Rabindranath Tagore

In our culture, we have learned to fear death as the cessation of life, the end of pleasure, of experience, of all that we know on this earth. Science has taught us to believe that human death is a terminal state, a state of oblivion, a void that swallows life up forever, depriving us of redemption or the chance to make amends.

When you "flatline" on the EEG, your heart stops beating and all brain activity ceases. This is the scientific definition of death.

Because it represents the end of everything, death is often seen, by those who suffer unbearable pain or anguish, as a release or an escape from their suffering. Death is a welcome sleep, a state of unconsciousness, the lack of a felt reality.

For others, however, death is not an end, nor is life just a beating heart and measurable brainwave activity. It is a training ground in which we learn the art of dying so that we can live again. For these people, life never dies.

Robert Thurman, in his translation of *The Tibetan Book of the Dead*, states that our scientific definition of death is neither accurate nor complete.

The illusion of the subjective "I" in the individual consciousness, assumed by materialists to correspond with the presence of brain wave activity, should cease with the cessation of brain waves. Yet the picture of death as a nothing in consciousness is not a scientific finding. It is a conceptual notion. There are many cases of people being revived after "flatlining" for some time, and they report intense subjective experiences. [1]

Thurman goes on to say that "a considerable body of credible evidence supports the probability of post-death existence of consciousness and sentient future life continuity." [2] In other words, there is life after death.

There have been many recorded statements of "near-death experiences" from people who were declared clinically dead and were revived. Many report the experience of being in a tunnel and moving toward a bright light. They are aware that they are about to "cross over" into another realm, and that this other realm represents death. They report feeling joy and relief, followed by disappointment when they are "yanked" back into life.

According to Dolores Cannon in her book *Between Death & Life: Conversations with a spirit*, "What they're describing is what they see up to the approach to the barrier between the physical and the spiritual ... this bright light is the barrier itself ..."[3]

When We Die

In order to understand what happens to us after we die, we need to understand the nature of energy and how it behaves.

According to the first law of thermodynamics, energy can neither be created nor destroyed. Nothing is new in the Universe. What we constantly see are different formations of the same atoms.

So it is with the cosmos. We are not separate from the world. Says David Staume:

> Although we perceive separate "things," they're like rain, steam, snow, rivers, and clouds—all water, all somewhere in the cycle of either issuing from or returning to the sea, and separate from it only in appearance ...
>
> Our wonderful cosmos is such a system, an indivisible system. Fortunately, no matter how poor our descriptions or weak our analogies, the two principles that arise from this are clear: first, nothing is in any sense truly separate from anything else; and second, the whole is enfolded in every part.[4]

Many things that were separate in the physical world merge in the astral world quite naturally.

Sight, hearing, taste, and smell, for example, emanate from the same place. So to hear is to see, to smell is to hear, and to see is to smell. Just as things previously seen as separate and distinct in the physical world have been revealed by physics to be facets of the same thing, such as matter and energy, space and time, waves and particles, so in the astral world, every part contains within it the wisdom of the cosmos.

Many psychologists and neurologists suspect that the electromagnetic field that is the mind, and can be identified as human thought processes, may well function independently of the brain. ~Migene González-Wippler

Our physical body is connected to our astral body by a silver cord that is a type of energy. When we die, and we go through the "bright light," that cord is severed because we are passing through an intense energy field. When we go through this energy barrier, we are aware of a bright energy that cleanses us and adjusts our spiritual vibrations to be compatible with the spiritual level we have attained.

Experiments indicate that the mind, or consciousness, is not a physical object like the brain. The brain receives information that the consciousness gathers and then proceeds to translate it into thoughts and ideas. But it's the consciousness that identifies, categorizes, and generally organizes the information received. It is also believed that this information processing function is independent of the constraints of time and space.

Once we are on the other side, we may see scenes that resemble things we remember on the physical plane, but they seem much more beautiful to us. Gradually we begin to realize that these are constructs of our own mind and we are seeing only what our minds are ready for. Eventually we are ready to see things as they truly are.

Planes of Existence

According to ancient teachings, there are seven planes of existence. The first plane is the material plane, the one we identify as our physical world. The second is the force plane, or etheric plane. Then comes the astral plane, followed by the fourth, or mental plane. Very little is known about the three planes that follow these except that they are believed to be of a high degree of spiritual evolution.

When a person dies, their spirit and their astral body go to one of the subplanes of the astral world where the spirit rests in a peaceful and regenerative sleep, during which it undergoes a cleansing and prepares for whatever place corresponds to its level of spiritual development. The astral body remains in the astral world for a brief time after the spirit leaves it. When the spirit awakens, it passes to the mental plane, from where it proceeds to its appropriate level.

> *You probably noticed, soon after the death of your body, that you hadn't gone anywhere in space—you were pretty much in the room you died in, or around about the bus that hit you ... all that actually occurred was that your consciousness changed focus. You were no longer focused in your physical body—you were focused in the body you have now. It's called your astral body, and the world it allows you to perceive is called the astral world.*[5]

Eventually, the astral body loses strength and disintegrates like the physical body. The more spiritually advanced a person is, the faster his or her astral body will disintegrate.

The Astral World

Migene González-Wippler in her book *What Happens After Death: Scientific & personal evidence for survival*, tells us:

> *In the astral world there are zones of great beauty and light that are occupied by higher spirits, but there are also places of darkness and terror inhabited by dark and destructive entities. These terrifying habitations have also been created by the mental vibrations and memories of the beings that inhabit them, most of whom committed terrible crimes and other destructive acts during their material lives.* [6]

Each plane of existence in the astral world has its own vibratory rate. The higher the plane, the faster will be its vibratory rate. The vibratory rate of a spirit depends on its evolutionary development and it will be in perfect harmony with the plane to which it belongs. Spirits are not able to ascend to a superior plane, where the vibrations are stronger and faster, but they can descend to a lower plane and remain there as long as they wish. According to most mystical schools, higher spirits descend to the lower levels of the astral plane to help the spirits who inhabit these darker regions seek redemption.

We enter the astral world, or Interlife, for a period of time in order to rest and learn. This is the time when we will evaluate where we have been and where we need to go next. Our actions in the life just past will be examined and measured against our karmic destiny. Have we learned the lessons of that destiny or must we repeat them? We don't do the journey alone—we are offered assistance in the form of spirit guides, who are able to consult with a council of higher spirits that meets in a council chamber in the center of a powerful energy field.

> *If you were to look at it with physical eyes it would appear that where we are gathered is suspended in midair, but it is really not. It is supported by an energy field that you cannot perceive with the eyes of your level. The energy field is a beautiful deep violet color and it surrounds all of us. There are not really any definite walls or ceilings; everything is just this deep violet and gold. And suspended in the center of this energy field is a council chamber, I suppose you would call it.*[7]

As we understand it—and journeys seem to prove it—members of this council have reached a more advanced plane than most, but have not yet attained the highest plane, that of total enlightenment. They work closely with those who guide individuals on the lower planes. These spirit guides see things as they appear on the physical plane, so they can help individuals plan their future path and make their choices.

In *Between Death & Life: Conversations with a spirit,* Cannon tells us this about the relationship between our decision making and the role of the council:

> *You are truly the master of your own fate and destiny. You, yourself, are in complete control*

*of what you call your lifetime. You are the one
who is making decisions as to when and where
and how. We [on the council], from our point
of view, can see all the options spread out
before you. But it is you, yourself who must
make the final decisions. You also cannot help
but influence other individuals while you are
living on this plane. You influence individuals
continuously.*[8]

Those on the council switch back and forth
between lifetimes, sometimes working on a general council and sometimes acting as a guide.
Those who are guides have usually served on the
general council and there is much interchange of
information between the two. It allows for greater
awareness as well as different perspectives.

Before we begin our return trip into the physical
life, we go through a series of planning sessions
with our guides and teachers. During this process,
we also check out the family we are considering
being born to in our next life on earth. Yes, we
choose our parents!

In chapter six of *The Book of the Soul*, Ian Lawton
gives us the graphic description of the process of
choosing lives during the Interlife, comparing it to
being in a theater and watching an interactive
movie:

*Here souls are able to review the various
options available to them in terms of a selec-
tion of human beings that will be incarnate
with more or less the right sort of aptitudes,
circumstances and environment, at about the
right time, perhaps in a number of geographic
locations. So effectively this place is one where*

the subject can manipulate time and control the movie telepathically as if it were a video playback, fast-forwarding where necessary and even pausing the scene to enter it temporarily and gain direct experience of that particular incarnation.[9]

The Soul / Body Agreement

We generally assume that when a woman becomes pregnant, most of the time the baby is born complete with soul, and that both mother and baby remain together for the journey through the chosen lifetime.

But it isn't always that way.

Sometimes the soul doesn't enter until after the child is born—occasionally as long as a few months after.

Sometimes the soul leaves after the start of the forming of the body, and a miscarriage occurs; sometimes the soul chooses a body that it knows will be aborted; and sometimes the soul makes the choice of leaving just before birth, or just after as in the case of SIDS (or Sudden Infant Death Syndrome). In those cases, the baby dies before it lives the life the parent expects.

How and why are these choices made? We know they are usually grief-ridden for the parents, whenever and however the choice is made—but what could possibly be the reason for such a choice by the soul?

Generally speaking, the soul doesn't actually join the body until the 12th or 13th week after conception—but there are exceptions to this.

Sometimes a soul is so eager to come in that it joins the mother at the time of conception. Sometimes the soul is so reticent that it doesn't join the baby until birth or after. The joining of the spiritual and physical is usually harmonious, but occasionally it can be tumultuous. Again, why should this be?

Palden Jenkins says in his article "Psychic Abortions" (1999):

> *No one knows the inner reasons, existing in their own right, which lie behind a soul's decision to be conceived, and to choose a specific set of parents. Therefore a key part of the process is to glean this from the soul itself. …*
>
> *Whatever decision is made (and this is open at the beginning of this process), the final decision, methinks, needs to come from the children / souls. It concerns what is the most realistically manageable and achievable evolutionary path forward, for them, and for the parents and for other closely-involved people, jointly and severally … The "abortion" is done by the child itself—usually within three or so days …*
>
> *In my experience, pre-birth and immediately post-birth souls are well capable of making fully aware life-decisions, especially if supported through it, but in the end it is the child-souls who choose whether or not to take on the challenges before them.* [10]

CHAPTER 3

Reincarnation and Life After Death

"Who are you?" said the Caterpillar.
Alice replied rather shyly, "I—I hardly know
sir, just at present—at least I knew who I was
when I got up this morning, but I must have
changed several times since then."
~Lewis Carroll

The belief in reincarnation, or the cyclical pattern of life and death as the continual flow of energy between all levels of existence, goes back thousands of years.

The ancient Egyptians may have been the first to believe in the immortality of the soul, and in the concept of reincarnation. A translation from an ancient Egyptian scroll tells us: "The soul warns, only if a man is allowed to continue evolving can the intellect reach the heart."

Hindu belief in reincarnation is well documented in the *Katha Upanishad* of India, dating back to the 6th Century BCE, which states:

The self ... does not die when the body dies. Concealed in the heart of all being lies the atma, the Spirit, the Self; smaller than the smallest atom, greater than the greatest spaces.

Death borders upon our birth, and our cradle stands in the grave.
~Joseph Hall (1574–1656)

Buddhist belief in the cycle of birth, death, and rebirth also dates back to the 6th Century BCE. Pre-Columbian civilizations such as the Aztecs, Mayans, and Toltecs believed that the dead could return at a later time, after having spent time in the afterlife. This time spent in the afterlife is what we call the Interlife, Bardo, or the Life Between Lives.

Rabbi Elie Kaplan speaks of how Jewish mystics traditionally view reincarnation as an opportunity to develop the soul.

> *In the study of Jewish text, I join a centuries-old conversation on the meaning of life and learn that, among the most sensitive and mystically oriented of my ancestors, many saw this world as only a passageway to another world. Reincarnation in the Jewish mystical literature was consistently viewed as real and as another opportunity to develop our souls. The Jewish tradition affirms that we have spirit guides, or visiting souls, that come to aid us on our spiritual path.* [1]

Hypnosis, when used appropriately, can reveal the existence of past lives. The therapeutic practice of past-life regression, as practiced by hypnotists and hypno-therapists, shows us the healing power of revisiting previous lifetimes and death experiences. Masses of data have been accumulated through the work of therapists such as Michael Newton, Dr. Joel Whitton, Irene Hickman, Hazel Denning, and Winafred Lucas.

Also well documented are children's detailed memories of former lives. These "memories" have been corroborated by others who were there at the time and stand up to the investigation of reputable researchers, such as Dr. Ian Stevenson. And, by the way, Dr. Stevenson didn't believe in using hypnosis to access past lives.

Ancient Knowledge of the Interlife

We can see from the writings that all of these ancient cultures also believed in the concept of an Interlife, or Life Between Lives, a place where the soul rests before journeying into the next lifetime to continue its learning. All of them saw the Interlife as a place of peace, pleasure, rest, and learning before they either evolved into higher realms or into other states of consciousness.

Hundreds of years before the time of Christ, Egyptian mythology told of an Interlife, and both the Hindu and Buddhist religions still believe in the Interlife or Bardo.

In the *Tibetan Book of the Dead*, a graphic presentation is given of how this process appears to the individual (Soul and / or Self) on passing through the Veil. Ormond McGill, in *Grieve No More, Beloved: The book of Delight*, writes that the Bardo is the realm of the lower astral planes where the soul is purged:

> *You have entered the shadowy borderland of the next world. It is a place of judgment, reflection and contemplation for the soul. Further, it is a place for decision to advance rapidly to higher planes or states of being or*

Such growth will move humans into ever-higher energy states, ultimately transforming our bodies into spiritual form and uniting this dimension of existence with the afterlife dimension, ending the cycle of birth and death.
~James Redfield

to seek rebirth for shortly re-entering the physical world. The choice will be yours but first you will stand before judgment of your SELF as revealed with the "Clear Light."[2]

Whether we call it Bardo, Interlife, or the "Blue Mist," the Interlife is the space between our current life and the one before, the time between death and re-entering the womb for another life. But what goes on in that time–space? What happens to the soul?

The first basic Bardo experience is the experience of uncertainty about whether one is actually going to die, in the sense of losing contact with the solid world, or whether one could continue to go on living. This uncertainty is not seen in terms of leaving the body, but purely in terms of losing one's ground; the possibility of stepping out from the real world into an unreal world.[3]

What do we learn, or more importantly, what do we need to learn from that time? Many writers, including those with Near Death Experiences, have documented the visions, the experiences that happen during those times. And they mostly follow similar patterns: the soul group, the learning process, the council of elders, the choice of the new body / life we make before re-entering this world.

Often, questions are answered:

- What are the key elements or purpose of my "thumbprint" Soul?

- Who are the people that I have journeyed with from lifetime to lifetime?

- What is the purpose of my journey in this lifetime?

- How and why did I choose this particular body and brain?

- Why is it so difficult for me to be happy?

- Who am I really?

- What is blocking my growth?

- Why is it hard for me to be loved?

- What agreements am I here to work out this time around?

Fascinating and profoundly moving questions and answers.

In hypnosis, a Life Between Lives session demonstrates that we live our current life by design, not by accident! It is our soul spirit and destiny review. This profound experience brings a deeper awareness and self-understanding of soul purpose and identity on earth. A new sense of empowerment emerges, providing a new vision, a stronger sense of self-direction, and energy for life.

CHAPTER 4

The Role of Karma

Repeated experiences lead to wisdom.
– Joseph J. Weed
Wisdom of the Mystic Master

Any discussion of the Interlife needs also to look at the concept of karma. Karma, loosely defined, is the Buddhist idea that what goes around comes around. Put another way, what we send into the universe comes back to us. We reap what we sow; we have to pay the consequences for our actions.

Karma is the cornerstone of reincarnation. The whole point of rebirth is to achieve enlightenment—the ability to love perfectly and have true inner peace. We do this by dealing with karma. Karma makes us responsible for our mistakes and unlearned lessons in this life as well as past lives. It's like a hand of cards that we are dealt and must decide how to play. We can choose to live with open eyes, on the lookout for the lessons karma has in store, ready to recognize and learn them. Or we can blindly stumble through, ignorant to the lessons. Our choice.

The concept of karma has been "pop-culturized" recently in the hit television sitcom *My Name is Earl*. The premise of the show is that thief, con artist, and generally scummy guy Earl Hickey wants to atone for his lifetime of wrongs. Earl wins the lottery and feels he doesn't deserve such good fortune, since he has spent his whole life doing wrong. He believes that all his misdeeds have created massive bad karma for him (despite his turn of good luck), and he wants to correct his mistakes in order to clear it. Earl makes a list of all the wrongs he has committed, and each episode of the show is built around his selecting an item from the list and going about correcting it.

> Karma will be seen as not expressing what you are, but what you have done to make you what you are.
> ~Ormond McGill

How Karma Works

To accept the idea that our actions in this life and in past lives can have an affect on us in the future, we have to accept the idea that actions carry energy. Doing good deeds—being friendly, smiling at a stranger—actions like these send out *good* energy or vibes. Flipping off a slow driver in the passing lane, "tasting" grapes while shopping at the supermarket, spreading gossip—these actions send out *bad* energy or vibes.

The vibes we send out through our actions don't just float into space and dissolve. They actually affect things. The energy of our actions is as real as a sound wave; we just don't currently have any real way to detect or "hear" it.

This energy can interact with the atmosphere and the matter inside the atmosphere. Proof of this is seen in the research of Masaru Emoto.

The Power of Thoughts

In his book, *The Messages of Water*,[1] Masaru Emoto studies the effect of projected thoughts and emotions on water molecules. His experiments involve observing the molecules in their original state, then doing things like labeling a bottle of water with the words "I love you" or "Thank you," or playing heavy metal music for a bottle of water, or praying beside a water sample. Afterwards, Emoto re-observes the molecules, noting any changes that have taken place.

His discoveries are astounding. In every case, the water that is exposed to positive vibrations forms crystals of the most intricate and beautiful designs. One sample that was treated with chamomile oil actually made crystals that mimicked the flower's form. Another sample taken from a Japanese dam appeared as a blob in the before picture, but after an hour-long prayer practice next to the dam, a new sample had molecules that looked like diamond snowflakes, glittering like crystals.

The water exposed to negative vibrations inevitably formed no crystals at all and instead became unstructured, chaotic, and dark. Frozen crystals broke in two when Elvis Presley's "Heartbreak Hotel" was played. A water sample labeled with the words "Adolf Hitler" returned no crystals, no snowflakes, no patterns whatsoever— just images of disorganized, frenzied whorls.

By photographing his water samples in the before and after states, Emoto provides visual proof again and again of two things. Not only do human thoughts and emotions have the ability to radiate out from the body, but also that these thoughts and emotions actually manipulate physical reality. This truth has extraordinary implications. Just think about it for a moment …

If our thoughts and words can *change the structure of water molecules*—if labeling a water sample with the words "I hate you" can distort its molecules—what happens when you say those words to another person? Especially considering the human body is 70 percent water? By the same token, what happens when you say the words "I love you"?

The point is simple and profound: the power of intention. Your words, your actions, thoughts, feelings—everything you say, think or do, carries with it the energy that created it. Not only that, those intangible vibrations influence the matter around them.

Putting all this into a more scientific frame, think back to high school physical science and Newton's third law of motion: for every action, there is an equal and opposite reaction. Newton was talking about the interaction of physical objects. But if we consider "action" in a larger sense—the transfer of energy on a physical, mental, or emotional level—then it's a scientific law that what we send out comes back to us, like a boomerang. What we think about—we bring about. Karma IS science.

The Law of Equilibrium is the pendulum of the cosmic clock—will pushing the pendulum one way and karma pushing it back, and so the cosmic clock ticks.
~David Staume

If you are agreeing with me in this book so far, you already know that you are more than your physical body. This is not a new idea—that the body is merely the housing for something larger, called the soul, or spirit, or aura. Some people call this the energy body—the field of energy that surrounds and permeates the physical body.

The energy body is like the body's memory. Just as the brain records and files events into a memory bank, the energy body does the same, except the memories are stored in the aura. This field contains and reflects your energy. It surrounds you and carries with you the emotional energy created, every positive and negative internal and external experience. This emotional force impacts the physical body with what we call the mind-body connection. In this way your experiences are the tapestry of your life—and they become your biology!

Every event, thought, and feeling is imprinted on your energy body, encoding it with information. This information can also affect the health of your cells.

The best-selling book *Anatomy of the Spirit*[2] by Caroline Myss illustrates just how profoundly our choices and actions can affect our lives. It tells the story of Julie, a woman with serious ovarian and breast cancer, who attended a healing workshop, hoping to learn how to heal her disease.

Julie was in a severely dysfunctional marriage. Her husband treated her with contempt. Their marriage had been celibate since the second year. After Julie's cancer diagnosis, her husband refused even to share a bed with her.

Julie's relationship with her husband was one humiliation after another. She was unable to claim any power in her life, to the point of refusing the treatment she needed because her husband didn't approve. She died within a year.

Julie's inability to recognize or claim any measure of personal power ultimately led to her death. Had she seen her illness as a learning opportunity, she might have been able to take some power for herself and learn an important life lesson.

Every human being is the author of his own health or disease. ~Buddha

This is exactly the kind of thing karma is made of. We are meant to learn certain things in each lifetime. Each of us has a unique set of lessons to learn. If we don't learn those lessons, we take them into the Interlife and into the next lifetime, at which point they become past-life lessons that we have to try to learn all over again.

For Julie, the lesson was one of self-respect and self-love. Her illness was the card that karma dealt her to help her learn. She was unable to learn that lesson, so Julie died with those unlearned impressions stamped all over her energy body. Her physical body was able to shut down and shed the impressions, but her energy body will carry that tainted energy field with it into the Interlife, and possibly future lives.

But always, we have to remember that her soul may have seen the learning in a different way—how she handled her life, from her soul's perspective, may have been appropriate. Although we can use Julie, and others that we know like her, as examples, we have to always bear in mind that, ultimately, no one of us on this planet at this time really knows it all! So we have to be gentle with our judgments and certainties and aware of our unknowing.

This is where karma comes in. We are not born and given life just because ... There is a greater spiritual purpose. We are all here to achieve enlightenment, the spiritual state of perfect peace and serenity. We incarnate on earth for as many lifetimes as it takes to learn the lessons we need to learn in order to grow into enlightenment.

Karma and the Interlife

When we think or worry about karma, it's usually how it relates to our current lifetime. This is the only lifetime that is significant and relevant to most people.

But this book is about the *Inter*life. How does karma relate to the Interlife?

It is during the Interlife that we choose the lessons we want to learn, analyze what went wrong in our last incarnation, and plan for the next lifetime so that we can ensure we have opportunities to settle what needs settling.

Some people refer to this process as the "soul contract." Think of soul contracts this way:

> *[Just imagine a] whole group of souls planning and preparing, some of which will have experienced many incarnations together. It is a beautiful, meticulously and intricately planned event each and every time a soul desires to re-incarnate ...*[3]

The reason we do this is to set up scenarios in which our soul can learn and grow. During the Interlife, we decide what lessons we need and

To accept the process of reincarnation is to accept that only by taking complete responsibility for ourselves can we hope to achieve rapid personal growth through the cycle of successive rebirths.
~Joel L. Whitton

want to learn. If there are leftover lessons from a previous lifetime that we were unable to learn, we write those into the new soul contract.

That's all karma is: the Universe's teacher, urging us toward the lessons we've chosen. I keep saying it's like a hand of cards that we are dealt. Every moment of life is a card in that hand. Every moment, we have the power to choose how we will play.

So, if we die as Julie did, the un-played cards—the unlearned karmic lessons—go with us, encoded into our energy. We carry them into every lifetime until the lifetime when we actually learn the lesson. We are meant to achieve the 10th soul level, and we keep getting cosmic do-overs until we do.

Karma and the Noble Truths

Buddha's Second Noble Truth says that karma is the root cause of suffering.

WHAT! So you're telling me that my suffering *is my own fault?*

Well, sort of.

It's true—your own actions do produce your karma, and your karma can produce your suffering. As we discussed earlier, you can choose to focus on the suffering and feel like you're being punished, or choose that the focus be to learn.

Hidden in this choice of focus is a magnificent opportunity for redemption and growth.

Karma means action that causes development and change, and so is close to what we mean by evolution.
~Tibetan Book of the Dead [4]

That opportunity is embodied in Buddha's Third Noble Truth: "The cessation of suffering, through which it is explained that the causes of karma and the defilements can be removed."

Yes: *The causes of karma can be removed.*

Whew! That's better!

OK. Let's go over it again.

Actions produce karma. Negative actions produce negative karma. Positive actions produce positive karma. So it follows that eliminating the negative actions will eliminate the negative karma.

It sounds so simple! You're thinking, "All I have to do is stop being unkind or selfish and my suffering will end?"

It *is* that simple—but not that easy.

There are three kinds of actions, and each kind of action is either virtuous or un-virtuous. The three categories of action are mental, verbal, and physical.

So karma is caused not just by good or bad actions, but good or bad thoughts and words, too. Which is good news and bad news! Considering how automatic our thoughts can be, how often and quickly we jump to speak, how habitual our negative feelings can be, the suggestion to simply stop being unvirtuous is a tall order.

But that is the challenge and purpose of karma to begin with: overcoming the difficulties we encounter in order to learn and grow. Karma "urges us to act, to overcome old habits, and to accept responsibility for ourselves today, despite the past."[5]

As we know, "the past" goes much further back in time than just this lifetime. The past stretches backwards into seemingly endless dimensions of past life. The knowledge that karma follows us not just through this lifetime but through many can be daunting.

So karma is like an eternal card game. Life after life, we are holding those cards and planning our moves. Sometimes we make good decisions and win the hand; sometimes we make bad decisions and win the hand in that life—but not in a karmic sense.

However we choose, we carry these decisions from lifetime to lifetime, recreating the same situations over and over until we learn from them, and release the energy and the Karma around that energy. Karma isn't a punishment but a lesson to learn as quickly or as slowly as we choose.

Again, *we choose* how we handle the karmic hand we're dealt. We can learn "as quickly or as slowly as we wish."

You may be thinking, "How am I supposed to choose to learn my lessons if I can't remember what I did wrong in the first place?!"

This is where past-life regression comes in. Whether the journeys are real or a metaphor that the mind makes up—it matters not. Whether we live in the past, present or future, or whether time

In the between-life state the soul reviews its performance across many lifetimes and chooses to resolve or atone for certain deeds in the next life.
~Joel L. Whitton

is all now, at one time ... again, it doesn't matter. What does matter is which part of ourselves we use in each lifetime. Are we kind? Are we harsh and thoughtless? Do we live a life of empty self-absorption, or do we take care of those around us? In each life there is a lesson to learn, and how we handle that lesson becomes our karma ... becomes what we take into our next ... or current lifetime.

The Four Powers

Once you remember the past actions that may have created your karma, perhaps the best news in all of this is that it is possible to clear and correct that karma, Earl Hickey-style. But even if you never have a past-life regression and you never remember anything about your previous incarnations, it is still possible to resolve negative karma and create positive karma for the future.

Buddhism calls the keys to clearing karma "The Four Powers of Purification."[6] Earl Hickey is a good example of each of the powers in action.

Power of the Object. Think of all beings you might have hurt. Earl did this when he made his list of wrongs. You don't have to know all the specifics—if you can't remember, just imagine. Chances are, whatever wrongs you have had done to you in this life are the wrongs that you did to others in a past life. Karma is nothing if not perfectly just.

Power of Regret. Feel sorrow for the negative actions you have done. This does not mean you should wrack yourself with guilt—guilt is always a waste of time and energy! You simply examine your actions and recognize that the negative ones were unwise. Earl shows his regret in every episode when he remembers the specific wrong he is trying to correct.

Power of Promise. This is where you promise not to repeat the negative actions. Sincerity is very important here. You can't really say you'll *never* do something again. We all make mistakes. But you have to put genuine effort into trying not to repeatedly make the same mistakes.

Power of Practice. Basically, doing good deeds is "good practice." Earl Hickey does a good deed in every episode for the person he wronged in the past. You can do the same!

So it's good news! We're not locked into our negative karma. We have the ultimate power to create good karma. It may not be easy. But the important thing is that it is possible.

A Parable[7]

In a time long ago, there was an old monk who, through diligent practice, had attained a certain degree of spiritual penetration.

He had a young novice who was about eight years old. One day, the monk looked at the boy's face and saw there that he would die within the next few months. Saddened by this, he told the boy to take a long holiday and go and visit his parents. "Take your time," said the monk. "Don't hurry back." He felt the boy should be with his family when he died.

Three months later, to his astonishment, the monk saw the boy walking back up the mountain. When he arrived, the monk gazed at the novice, and saw the boy would now live to a ripe old age.

"Tell me everything that happened while you were away," he said. So the boy told the story of his journey down from the mountain. He told of villages and towns he passed through, of the rivers crossed and the mountains climbed.

Then he told how one day he came upon a stream in flood. He noticed, as he tried to pick his way across the flowing stream, that a colony of ants had become trapped on a small island formed by the flooding stream. Moved by compassion for these poor creatures, he took a branch of a tree and laid it across one flow of the stream until it touched the little island. As the ants made their way across, the boy held the branch steady, until he was sure all the ants had escaped to dry land. Only then did he continue on his way home. "So," thought the old monk to himself. "That is why the gods have lengthened his days."

This parable is a beautiful metaphor for the ultimate goal of karma, reincarnation, the Interlife, and all of it. We each have unique lifetimes; we each have individual lessons to learn—but the unifying thread in every human life is the goal of perfect love and perfect peace. The monk's novice felt a love and respect for all life so profound that he rescued a colony of ants from certain death. Most people would not only not *save* the ants, they wouldn't even notice them trapped by the flood in the first place.

So let's not continue thinking that karma is some sort of dominatrix following us around for all eternity, making sure we suffer! Karma is more like a tough-love mom, holding us to the consequences of our actions and choices until we see the right way to behave. Karma wants us to learn and grow so that we can feel the kind of love the monk's apprentice felt for all living things. That kind of boundless, all-encompassing love is the human soul in its purest, most powerful and peaceful state.

This is why karma clings to us until we learn. All we have to do is see it, understand it, and act in the interests of preserving the best of it. If we do that, all of our lives are transformed.

Even death is not to be feared by one who has lived wisely.
~Buddha

CHAPTER 5

Your Soul and Soul Mate

A soul mate is someone who has the locks to fit our keys, and the keys to fit our locks.
~Richard Bach

There are two overarching questions around relationships that people always want answered. The questions go something like this: "Is there a perfect mate out there for me?" or "Will I meet my soul mate?"

When most people think of soul mates, they are thinking in terms of "forever," "life partner," and "two halves of one whole." People think a soul mate is their one and only true love. But in reality, this type of connection is shared between "twin flames," not soul mates. I'll talk about twin flames a little later on—although they're not really part of the soul circle.

As human beings, we instinctively yearn for this kind of intimate connection with another. For most people, if we're not happily partnered, then we're looking to be happily partnered. We're always on the lookout for that one person who will "complete" us.

Love makes
your soul crawl
out from its
hiding place.
~Zora Neale
Hurston

However, meeting our "soul mate" is not always synonymous with meeting our life partner or lover.

Soul mate relationships are not necessarily romantic relationships, and, almost always, there is more than one. Soul mate relationships are common and plentiful. You could come across ten or twenty (or more) soul mates in your lifetime! These soul mates are considered by many to be part of your soul circle or soul group. And your soul circles travel together with you through many lifetimes.

Soul Circles and Soul Mates

The soul circle plays an integral role in the Interlife and in the overall journey of each individual soul. Every person "has a group of souls we are spiritually connected to ... a group we are meant to connect with in both the spirit world, and here by choice in physical form."[1]

Remember from our discussion of the Interlife journey, that our whole purpose for incarnating on earth is for spiritual growth. This is also the reason we are tied to a soul circle. Members of a soul circle enact soul contracts and agree to meet again on earth. They "come into our lives at seemingly random times, but in fact these meetings were prearranged between us in spirit before we came here. We agree to connect and enable each other to learn a lesson or many lessons."[2]

Very often the first or second stop in the Interlife journey is the meeting with the soul circle. This is where we reconnect with our soul mates. There is an overwhelming feeling of joy and peace when we meet again after our physical death. These souls sometimes remain with us during the Interlife journey, welcoming us when we arrive, guiding us through the journey, supporting us through our life review.

The following excerpt is from a book on the near-death experience of a sailor who reports the experience of meeting his soul group in the Interlife. I've included such a large excerpt because the richness of detail he shares really crystallizes the purpose of the soul group and the experience of meeting our soul mates.

> *The light in itself was the most beautiful vision you can imagine. I wasn't wanting for any-thing else to look at.*
>
> *Yet, in the light, I noticed three other light fragments that became brighter. They had sil-houette shapes. Not clearly defined but I recognized them as other beings. It seemed like they were separating themselves from the light and coming to me. As they did, I could sense them projecting "welcome home" as if we were family and that there was joy in our reunion. I never had those strong feelings in life. This felt stronger and more binding than anything I had experienced in my life. I was now home, together with these beings. Since then, I have come to call them my Soul Group or Soul Family.*

They were so excited to be there and to see me. I can not express enough how they felt like family to me. I just knew I was home, and it felt so wonderful. They were supporting me and helping me by projecting waves of love and compassion. I was overcome with joy and the feeling of finally belonging somewhere and not isolated anymore. Beyond the original three, there were more light beings coming and joining us. They didn't really communicate, at least not in a way that you and I are accustomed to. There were maybe a dozen in all. Some of them were behind others so I couldn't see them as clearly as the ones closest to me, but they were all around me. These others were like family, but not as close as the first three. The first three were the prominent ones, like best friends or immediate family.

Beyond the group's support, I was also aware of the consciousness of the Light. When I think of God, I think of this consciousness of the Light. It almost seemed like there were billions and billions of Souls attached to that consciousness. I had a complete understanding of it when I was there, but now it is beyond my definition. I can tell you this. It was observing, supporting and an incredibly loving constant during my experience.

Along with not having a physical body, I was there without my life's drama wrapped around me. All the fiction I had created in my life of who I thought I should be was stripped away because the consciousness of the Light knew me better than I knew myself. I experienced my true self.[3]

The sailor's experience is true to the experiences of so many others—the feeling of being welcomed by family, the happiness, the light. Another detail that is true to the universal experience of soul groups and the Interlife is the fact that the sailor came away from the experience having learned some important lessons: acceptance and tolerance.

The major purpose of soul groups is to help each individual soul learn and grow. That's why we're here. That's why we contract to meet each other again. Sometimes these relationships are happy; sometimes they are less than happy. Either way, soul mate relationships are meant to teach us.

Often, people think a soul mate relationship is by definition a romantic love relationship. Sometimes this is true; sometimes it's not. Soul mates can incarnate as friends, family, or total strangers.

What Is a Soul Mate?

Many clients who come into our clinic are interested in finding their soul mate because—in their mind—a soul mate relationship has been represented in books, magazines, television, and movies as two people immersed in the bliss of a deep love experience—and that's what they believe. Even those already in a relationship wonder if their partner is a soul mate, assuming it is the most profound heart connection they can find. Sometimes it is. Sometimes it isn't.

But, contrary to popular belief, soul mate relationships are not the simple, glorious nirvana they are depicted to be. These relationships have captured our attention because they are filled with passion and growth, and therefore seem romantic. However, soul mate relationships can be quite painful, despite—or because of—the frenzy of passion.

Understand, soul mates are ideal partners because they are souls who contracted to spend time together during their current incarnation. However, soul mates are also the most challenging relationships because they are purposely established to stimulate growth.

Soul mate contracts are carefully discussed and initiated between future mates prior to their physical experience, during the Interlife, just as parental contracts are determined as you select the genetic pool and family environment which best support and maximize learning during your incarnate experience. This means that soul mate contracts are often designed to assist you in experiencing lessons that are difficult.

You pick relationships with souls that can best stimulate your growth based on a strong karmic connection. In fact, it is likely you will have issues left to resolve from prior lifetimes together. Or, you and your soul mate might be well suited for resolving a key emotional issue you have resisted learning in the past. A soul mate is perfectly designed to push your buttons so he or she can boost you into new realms of realization.

Quite often you will feel a pull towards that person which surpasses any emotional connection you could possibly have built up in the short time you have known them.
~Rachel Keene

Soul mate relationships are recognized by the passion they engender—otherwise, most human beings would never have the fortitude to connect or remain with these mates; the interaction is often fraught with fiery conflict or spurts of sexual passion. This passion is the glue that holds the union together as the two people work through the resolution of negative karma. It is the insurance that holds soul mates together during a roller-coaster ride through the heights of passion and the plunge to despair until the karmic work is completed.

When soul mates first meet, they sometimes feel as if they already know each other. They may feel very familiar to each other. Soul mate relationships may last a lifetime, and others may only be for a particular purpose and be temporary.

Regardless, all relationships serve a purpose and should be honored and appreciated for what they have to offer you in your personal spiritual growth. Thank the person and the experiences for all that you have had the opportunity to learn and clear. Know that ALL relationships are sacred, because they bring us closer to the Light of All That Is.

So Who Is Your Soul Mate, Then?

Again, a soul mate is any person who comes into your life for a short or a long period of time to help you learn a lesson that will advance your spiritual growth. Period. A soul mate can be your father, your sister, your friend, your boss, your dentist, or the guy you buy your paper from every morning.

Soul mates pre-arrange their encounters in the space between lives. One soul agrees to help another soul evolve in a certain way by learning a particular lesson. When both souls are incarnated, they meet to carry out their agreement. You don't have to worry about finding your soul mate. You will naturally find each other. This phenomenon is called the soul mate contract. Meeting a soul mate is not a random event—it is an officially pre-arranged ordeal.

> Before we ever even enter into any particular life cycle on this planet, there is a process beforehand that will more or less guide you through your entire life ... There are intricate plans made, and within those plans there are back-up plans created—several, in fact.[4]

Included within those plans and back-up plans are sub-contracts, so to speak, that you create with your soul mates. These soul mate contracts ensure that the two of you will meet in the next lifetime.

So, once you do meet a soul mate, how do you know you will *know* them? The very nature of a soul mate relationship ensures that you'll connect with the person at the right time, so this is not a matter of grave concern. There's no way you'd brush by a soul mate on the subway and never meet again. The fact that you are contracted with that person is an ironclad guarantee that you will meet and benefit each other in some way. But there is more than this cosmic explanation for why you are drawn to your soul mates. It's called the limbic brain.

I have learned silence from the talkative, tolerance from the intolerant and kindness from the unkind. I should not be ungrateful to those teachers.
~Kahlil Gibran

The Limbic Brain

The limbic system is a network of nerves and glands within the human brain that "is a major center for emotion formation and processing, for learning, and for memory."[5]

The limbic system is like a primitive memory bank. It stores memories and emotional connections that occur from birth to age three. It's where each of our unique emotional blueprints is formed. The information processed there becomes the basis for our emotional reality.

Children are the most absorbent sponges nature ever created. Babies and children are rampantly observing the connections among the adults who surround them. Until a child reaches age three, the limbic system is busy cataloging and recording every event into this memory bank.

> Children require guidance and sympathy far more than instruction.
> ~Annie Sullivan

Infants instinctively know that their caregivers are meant to treat them with love, dignity, and deep caring. They know on some level that they are helpless, and they rely on their caregivers to meet all their needs, both physical and emotional. They assume, following this primitive logic, that whatever type of care they receive represents what love truly is.

So these early experiences become models. We intuitively seek out whatever model we've assimilated into our subconscious. If our parents were distant and undemonstrative, we quickly take distant and undemonstrative as our definition of love. If our parents argued a lot, we learn that arguing means love. It becomes our karmic duty to settle these issues by working through them in our own relationships.

Encoded into our very brain is a pattern of behavior that we constantly try to recreate. This is where our soul mates come in.

I Felt an Instant Connection!

Many times I've had people tell me about someone they've met or maybe seen across the proverbial crowded room. They tell me about the instant connection they felt with this person, or how it seems like they knew the person already. They are convinced these are the signs of a soul mate relationship. My belief, however, is that this is rarely the case.

Instead, these instant connections are simply the intuitive recognition of a familiar pattern. It's the limbic brain at work.

When we meet someone and feel an instant connection, it's usually because they carry out the pattern that matches our definition of love. Even though the person may not have uttered a single word or exhibited a single indicative behavior, we know at a DNA level that they are a pattern match.

Soul mates are the people who come into our lives to help us resolve old patterns. Let's face it—most of us are not brought up with perfect and pristine models of love. Most of us have old wounds that are rooted in these early relationships. It is our spiritual goal to overcome such wounds. Our soul mates help us do it.

In his book *The Little Soul and the Sun*, Neale Donald Walsch allows a little soul to learn forgiveness in its next reincarnation. When the little soul asks how he can learn forgiveness if there is no one to forgive, another soul steps forward and offers to be the teacher. The little soul is amazed that a being of light would do this for him.

> *"Don't be so amazed," said the Friendly Soul, "you have done the same thing for me. Don't you remember? Oh, we have danced together, you and I, many times. Through the eons and across all the ages have we danced. Across all time and in many places have we played together. We have both been All of It. We have been the Up and Down of it, the Left and the Right of it. We have been the Here and the There of it, the Now and the Then of it. We have been the male and the female, the good and the bad—we have been both the victim and the villain of it. Thus we have come together you and I, many times before; each bringing to the other the exact and perfect opportunity to Express and to Experience Who We Really Are."*[6]

Your soul contract ensures you'll meet, and your limbic brain helps you recognize who they are.

Remember, soul mates can be anyone, not just romantic partners. They can be friends, siblings, coworkers, even a virtual stranger you only meet for one day. Anyone who comes into your life and pushes your emotional buttons in any significant way is likely a contracted soul mate you agreed to connect with in this lifetime.

If your soul mate is your romantic partner, it can be truly wonderful. But even if your partner isn't a soul mate, you can still have a deep, soulful connection that helps both of you grow. In fact, mutual growth should be a fundamental part of any love relationship.

Pizza or a Gourmet Meal?

Soul mate relationships are preparatory for the main event ... the "perfect partner." A soul mate contract simply indicates that you ordered the relationship prior to arrival. It is like a pizza delivery. You ordered it ahead of time so you could eat it when it arrived. However, it is not a five-course gourmet meal—i.e., a perfect partnership—that you are meant to slowly savor.

Recognize the preparatory work you have done in order to align with a perfect partner in balance, harmony, mutual uplifting, and love. For this is your final goal. Ultimately, when you connect with your perfect partner, you are ready to connect in a relationship that has the capacity to move both you and your mate to Divine Union between each other and with the Universe.

The Perfect Partnership

The learning experience derived from soul mates, if the work is done properly, is an excellent catalyst for moving toward a more evolved level of relationship. A perfect partnership has no karma attached to it. This means there are no prior imbalances from previous lifetimes together to resolve. The partnership is a mature one, characterized by balance because both players are

> The people we are in relationship with are always a mirror, reflecting our own beliefs, and simultaneously we are mirrors, reflecting their beliefs. So ... relationship is one of the most powerful tools for growth.
> ~Shakti Gawain

supporting the growth of themselves and each other without any resolution of past conflicts.

We have been led to believe that finding a soul mate is critical because it is our one and only ideal mate for this lifetime. If it is appropriate to your lifetime's experience, you will remain in your relationship with your soul mate past the point of resolution of karmic issues, evolving the soul mate contract into a partnership contract. But if it is not supporting your life experience, you will be impelled to move to new relationships.

Divorce is actually an institution designed for a soul's fast growth, not the anathema of the family structure it is often positioned to be. Divorce allows you to complete a soul mate contract and evolve to the next relationship. The longer you hold onto an inappropriate old relationship, because you know it and are familiar with it and are afraid that nothing new will surface, the less you will be likely to eventually evolve into the most pleasant relationship of all—a partnership relationship.

Subsequent relationships are often characterized by less frenzied passion but deeper love because one grows and matures through the earlier experiences. Plus, the subsequent relationships usually have fewer karmic ties. You are not resolving past lifetime conflicts or moving through a multitude of current lessons in a perfect partnership. You are simply partnering with a mate to experience the balance made possible through your prior relationship work.

This does not mean later relationships lack romance, or that you have grown old and lost your capacity for passion. It simply means the intensity of the passion experienced in earlier relationships will be less necessary as you move into unions based on mutual support through trust and friendship.

Twin Flames

Twin flames are very different from soul mates, and are very rare. Twin flames are two people in two separate bodies that share the same soul. Twin flames meet each other in their first incarnation so that they remember the soul frequency of the other being. They are then usually reunited during their last time on this planet. If twin flames meet before they are ready, they can be the total opposite and not at all compatible. When twin flames meet and are ready for each other, it is the most enjoyable experience possible on Earth.

At this point, twin flames are almost identical. They truly complement each other, and it is a hardship for them to be apart. For an outside observer, it is sometimes hard to distinguish the two people. They have a very strong bond and often have telepathy with each other. Their lives, even before meeting each other, have many parallels. Again, meeting your twin flame is very rare on this planet.

Rescinding Soul Mate Contracts

Yes, it's possible! But why would you want to break apart a soul contract?

Maybe you have decided to enter a lifetime with no soul mate contracts, since this type of relationship is not pertinent to your chosen lessons. You are literally a free agent who can choose the relationships that feel best. However, if you have experienced soul mate relationships prior to meeting your life partner, it is imperative to formally break those soul contracts.

Think of people you know who have broken up with a mate but seem unable to let go of the relationship. It impacts their emotional balance, and it flavors their life well past the point of separation. This is because the soul mate contract is still in place. The soul mate contracts were not broken when the karmic work was completed.

Soul mate contracts are established in the Akashic or soul records based on vows that have been taken at a soul level. The vows must be rescinded to feel a release, in order to move to the next experience—both emotionally and spiritually—be it another relationship or a time of solitude. In fact, if your vows are not rescinded, you may very well encounter the same individual in another lifetime based on the continued existence of the Akashic record contract. This is why some of you have entered relationships that did not feel quite right, yet you felt compelled to experience them. You are probably replaying a soul mate contract left over from a prior lifetime.

This is not to say that you cannot learn from these experiences, since every situation brings growth. However, this unfinished business detains you from intended relationships.

If you have been in a prior soul mate arrangement and feel you are not emotionally and spiritually released from it, it is time to rescind your vows. It is also appropriate to rescind your vows if you are currently in a soul mate relationship that is characterized by ongoing drama, the upheaval of passion followed by conflict, resolution of conflict, more passion, and more resolution, and you can't seem to stop the cycle.

The disavowal of your soul mate contract does not mean you will no longer be together. It simply removes the karmic pull from your interactions with your partner, which smoothes the friction in the relationship.

If you wish to end a soul contract, I have provided instructions in Addenda A, "How to Rescind a Soul Contract," at the end of this book.

Finding Your Soul Circle

One of the most amazing things about the other-worldly realm is that it's accessible to us even while we are still alive on earth. It is not necessary to die a physical death in order to visit there, meet our soul group, and gain knowledge about our life's higher purpose. Hypnotherapy is one way to access this sacred place within ourselves. I have provided a Soul Circle Meditation Script for self-recording in Appendix B at the end of this book,

The real voyage of discovery consists not in seeing new landscapes, but in having new eyes.
~Marcel Proust

so even if you don't have access to a regression facilitator, you can use self-hypnosis or meditation to tune in to the spiritual realm.

Soul mate and soul circle relationships are the most challenging and the most spiritually rewarding relationships you'll ever have. The friend who demeans you, the boyfriend who cheats, the mother who is somehow both overbearing *and* distant—these kinds of maddening relationships are usually the most significant ones, because they force you to look honestly at yourself, who you believe yourself to be, and what you really need and want in a relationship for your future.

As human beings, our greatness lies not so much in being able to remake the world as in being able to remake ourselves. ~Mahatma Gandhi

Soul mate relationships aren't always romantic in nature, and sometimes they don't last an entire lifetime. But this is not a detriment—soul mates are meant to help you learn a lesson. Once they've done what they came to do, they go. If you are in a spiritual frame of mind, you can be aware of this when it's happening, which will help you accept and appreciate whatever terms the soul mate contract requires.

Your soul circle is with you eternally. Some souls learn everything they need to learn and are able to "ascend" into a new circle with more advanced lessons. Some soul mates will skip a lifetime and appear in your next. Whatever the circumstance, these are the most valuable relationships you will ever have. They literally make you who you are. Soul circle relationships are sacred and powerful. As are you!

CHAPTER 6

Heaven and Hell on Earth

To different minds, the same world is a hell,
and a heaven.
~Ralph Waldo Emerson

Hell on earth is a given right now. Practically everywhere you look, you can see evidence of the ghastly state so much of the world is in. And so it has been for a while.

Ask anyone who has been through the Holocaust about hell on earth, or survivors of the Bosnian war, or Darfur. Ask the starving in Bangladesh. Look at the children who are brutally abused by their own parents, or the women who are routinely and ritually mutilated. Look at the cruelty to animals that is beyond understanding, or the lowest, deepest forms of depression, or the mindless, psychotic destruction of life. Surely these must count as hell on earth.

Heaven on earth is also a given right now. The times we see the sun come up over a mountain, or set and dip below a peaceful ocean, we exhale,

In the final
analysis, the
hope of every
person is simply
peace of mind.
~Dalai Lama

"This is heaven." When I mountain-trekked in the Kooteneys, I'd turn a corner on the path and see before me mountains stacked up, one behind the other, covered in grasses and flowers of colors not seen at sea level; hawks and eagles circling overhead; the sky, clear, bright, vivid blue; ancient rocks sharing their solid-state energy and the sound of quiet. Silence. Peace and beauty. Heaven on earth. For me. At that time. I still remember it in my heart-mind.

The blossoming of trees and flowers each spring. The giggle of little girls. A crying, ongoing belly laugh with my sister and friends. The purr of a cat on a lap, or the wet nose of a dog in the hand. Eyes that welcome with love. Each morning I awake healthy, with a new day to enjoy. This is my heaven!

I have often wondered if, in fact, our Interlife, as our heaven and hell, is right here, right now, at this time, on this planet.

Interlife on Earth

Isn't all of life a series of little deaths and rebirths? We are all constantly in a state of flux. Part of me believes that during times of great introspection, we are, in fact, in Bardo. Think about it. When do the most profound spiritual changes take place in our lives?

During a "dark night of the soul," there is nowhere to go but toward the light. Our spirit is at its most vulnerable. Everything is stripped away, and we are naked in the face of our weakness. The very nature of a rock-bottom moment, such as the turning point for an alcoholic or drug addict, is that we finally realize how far we have fallen and how far we have to go. There is so much pain, withdrawal, and searching for truth. The yearning has a fierce power. We know that we have a lesson, perhaps many lessons that we have to learn. Could this condition be Bardo?

Bardo, or the Interlife, remember, is the place we go between lives to refuel, refocus, heal, and redirect our spiritual growth. We come out of it when we are reborn into a fresh new life, one pregnant with possibilities for healing and evolution.

Isn't this exactly what happens when we reach the deepest depths of depression or depravity or desperation? There is nowhere to go but up, and the process of coming out of such a state brings the opportunity for innumerable spiritual lessons. This is the very definition of a soul's rebirth. It is the time of life lessons, the time for future growth planning, the time for a soul's shift back into the light.

This is the equivalent of the Interlife journey. Our souls are wiped clean and have the chance to start over.

We see it many times in classical literature and in history, the rebirthing of the human soul into another manifestation after a tragedy.

> Life is a process of becoming, a combination of states we have to go through. Where people fail is that they wish to elect a state and remain in it. This is a kind of death.
> ~Anais Nin

Dante and the Interlife

One famous and superb example of this theme can be found in Dante's *Inferno*, written in 14th century Italy. *Inferno* is an epic poem depicting Dante's allegorical journey through the underworld.

Inferno is a story that exists on two levels. One is the literal level, where the actions and images are taken at face value. The other level is purely symbolic, and all the major details actually represent something else, something bigger.

From the first scene of *Inferno*, the poem is rich with symbolism. The poem opens on the evening of Good Friday. As Dante is following a dark path through the forest, he loses his way. He can see the sun through the tops of the trees and tries to find his way out of the woods, but his path is blocked by three beasts. Dante retreats back into the forest full of fear.

> *Midway in our life's journey, I went astray from the straight road and woke to find myself alone in a dark wood.*

A dark path, a lost traveler, obstacles blocking his way to the light—do you see a theme developing here?

Dante meets a guide—the ghost of Virgil, the great Roman poet—who has come to help Dante find his way. Virgil tells him they will have to travel through hell in order to get to heaven.

Again, the theme.

Virgil leads Dante into hell. Dante witnesses tortured souls who are trapped in a sort of pre-limbo, being chased and bitten by hornets for all of eternity.

According to Dante, hell is organized into nine circles. Each circle houses sinners who committed progressively worse crimes. The first circle, for example, is for pagans who never knew Christ—a relatively minor sin. The next seven circles house souls who "specialized" in one of the seven deadly sins. The ninth circle is for the most depraved souls of all— betrayers of trust.

Abandon hope, all ye who enter here.

Dante goes through all eight circles and comes to the ninth, where he finds himself in the absolute lowest region of hell. It's an icy lake in which sinners stand frozen. Dante observes several sub-circles inside the ninth circle and then sees a huge shadowy figure before him. It is Lucifer himself, waist-deep in ice. Virgil and Dante have to climb down Lucifer's massive form in order to get out of hell. They emerge on Easter morning just before sunrise.

Again with the theme! Dante has to reach the deepest pits of hell, even touch the devil himself, in order to cross into sunlight. Even better, he emerges on Easter Sunday, a holiday that, for a Christian—which he was—celebrates resurrection and new life. Does this sound like the quintessential dark-night-of-the-soul journey?

The symbolism is clear: Sometimes you have to reach the very bottom, the worst possible place, before you can emerge cleansed and victorious. This theme is embodied in the last lines of the poem, which read:

> To get back up to the shining world from
>   there
> My guide and I went into that hidden
>   tunnel ...
> Where we came forth, and once more saw
>   the stars.

This theme of symbolic death and rebirth has been written and recorded in Western culture since well before the fourteenth century. In 800 BCE, Homer wrote the classical Greek epic, *The Odyssey*, in which the hero, Odysseus, undergoes several symbolic deaths and rebirths in his spiritual voyage toward enlightenment.

More recently, movies have picked up the theme. In *Revenge of the Sith*, part three of the Star Wars saga, the themes of birth, death, and rebirth are interwoven—Padmé's life ends as her children, Luke and Leia, are born and Anakin is subsumed into Darth Vader. The end of one cycle (the death of the Republic) leads to the beginning of another (the birth of the Empire). Terry Gilliam's 1991 film, *The Fisher King*, with Robin Williams and Jeff Bridges, has Bridges' character descend into the hell of an emotional breakdown before he can redeem (and resurrect) himself by helping the Robin Williams character find love again after the devastating death of his wife.

The important point to take from this theme is that we have the power to transform our lives in the here and now. We can bring ourselves out of hell and into the light again. This is the exact goal of the Interlife, animated on earth.

If each of us is living in the Interlife right now, what do we do with that information? If the point of the Interlife is to encourage and prompt spiritual growth, and the Interlife is right now, how do we approach that challenge?

It comes down to creating your own heaven or hell—creating your own Interlife.

The Power of Perspective— Through a simple metaphor

You are walking through the park one morning and come upon a young couple having a breakfast picnic. They are lost in their own world, canoodling and kissing in the grass.

Just before your walk, your partner blew up at you for leaving a towel on the bathroom floor. You are still seething with repressed anger and resentment. There's a part of you that feels as though your relationship is disintegrating.

So, coming across this young couple when you are in that state of mind, your immediate reaction is one of dismissal. "Get a room," you think. Or, you silently smirk at the thought that in a relatively short amount of time, their blissful union will probably end.

On the other hand, maybe you're taking this walk after breakfast in bed, made lovingly for you by your partner, who still adores you after many years together.

You and I are essentially infinite choice-makers. In every moment of our existence, we are in that field of all possibilities where we have access to an infinity of choices.
~Deepak Chopra

So when you come across the young couple, you think, "How wonderful it is to be young and in love." You finish your walk with a little spring in your step, thinking of your partner waiting for you at home.

This example speaks to the power of mental and spiritual perspective.

> The mind is its own place, and in itself, can make heaven of hell, and a hell of heaven.
> ~John Milton

In other words, your experience on earth is entirely up to you. The things that happen to you may be random, but the way you react is fully in your power. And it is your reaction to life that determines whether you walk every day in heaven or in hell.

Choosing Heaven

Heaven is all about the state of mind you choose. There is nothing inherently wrong with reacting to life's challenges in anger, fear, or sadness. Those are natural human emotions. But dwelling in these negative energies does nothing but attract more negativity.

The key to owning your perspective lies in your ability to center yourself and connect to your natural sense of peace and balance. If you are able, at any given moment, to "shake it off," whatever "it" is, and let go of the old and move forward into the peace within yourself, you will be creating an oasis inside of you where only goodness can dwell.

This kind of inner silence allows you to tune in to that still, small voice that lives in each of us. This voice guides and balances you. It is the voice of your higher self, of Spirit, of God—however you choose to name it. When you are able to hear this voice, you can see clearly. You can make right decisions. You can follow your heart. Even more than that, you can see each little insignificant moment of life for the beauty and majesty it contains. This is the definition of heaven on earth.

Mastering the ability to hear the voice is paradoxically the easiest and most difficult thing you can undertake. The voice is eternal and pervasive; it is always with you. But it is easy to get lost in the dust and noise of your—guilt—anger—resentment—shame—that can get in the way. Learning to slough away this negativity takes conscious choice and dedication. And often, when you're cruising smoothly along with your new, peaceful, heavenly soul, you think you've done all the spiritual work you'll ever need to do—and then something will happen that plunges you right back to where you started, and you'll think you never learned anything to begin with! It happens to us all.

Achieving heaven on earth is an ongoing process. It takes constant work and dedication. Like weight loss, you can't just stop once you reach your goal. Otherwise, you'll backslide. Spiritual peace requires regular maintenance, because there will always be factors that seem to prey on that peace. It's a continuous series of decisions.

When you finally choose this path, you will be living out the goal of the Interlife. If you choose to walk in peace and see each "problem" as an

Love is what we are born with. Fear is what we have learned here. The spiritual journey is the unlearning of fear and the acceptance of love back into our hearts.
~Marianne Williamson

The universe is transformation; our life is what our thoughts make it.
~Marcus Aurelius

opportunity for healing, you are living in the ideal state. You will be creating your own good karma—creating your own heaven on earth.

Heaven on Earth in Every Moment

We can experience heaven on earth as being here and now, in this moment and in successive moments of Now. Yesterday, I was out walking in the morning and I suddenly stopped and became present to and aware of everything. I was fully in the here and now.

> *We have to try to get rid of the notion of time. And when you have an intense contact of love with nature or another human being, like a spark, then you understand that there is no time and that everything is eternal.*
> *~Paulo Coelho*

Each of us has the ability to simply stop and be here and now in each and every moment. Why don't you just do that right now? Stop reading this. Look up and out into the world. Be present.

Notice the sounds, the smells; observe what's around you, your thoughts, your emotions. Be aware of being aware. You can do this at any time under any circumstances.

Make your heaven on earth, where you are, right now ... always.

CHAPTER 7

Mapping the Journey

Whenever I prepare for a journey
I prepare as though for death.
Should I never return, all is in order.
~Katherine Mansfield

As an ex-journalist, I have always carried just a little skepticism when working with past lives ... and now here I am faced with the prospect of facilitating clients' journeys through the Interlife.

In my research, I've discovered that many of the writers and researchers working with past lives and the Interlife seem to come up with the same journey, although they use different processes to enable clients to get there. It's amazing how, although the facilitation process differs, most often the end result is the same. Let me show you what I mean.

MICHAEL NEWTON

Michael Newton is a pioneer in the field of recorded Interlife research. He developed the concept and promotion of Life Between Lives and has been using it as a therapeutic tool for over 30 years. Newton calls his method "trance." Which is what I call hypnosis.

The purpose of using trance, or hypnosis, is to relax the mind so that it will more readily accept the images and impressions that arise from such relaxation. This is called Hypnotic Regression, and it helps people "recover memories locked within the mind that are difficult or impossible to specifically recall during waking consciousness."[1] Also, the openness of the mind "can be effectively channeled to promote positive and wanted change within individuals."[2]

During trance, people describe a shift from a psychological focus related to the conscious mind to a spiritual focus related to the soul's memory. Soul memory covers an infinite span of time.

The Newton system guides the client through the current life, one past life, and then through the womb into the Interlife. All the while, he makes sure the client is deeply into hypnosis so that the ego can be bypassed. The Interlife "is a very specific place the soul goes after each life to rest and discuss what the next incarnation should be."[3]

Newton helps people explore this place in a process that is like "opening the doors to the library of the soul's 'eternal' memories."[4] Despite the diversity of his clientele, they describe the Interlife in intimate detail, and Newton discovered over the years that they were all describing essentially the same process:

- How it feels to die
- What you see and feel right after death
- Meeting spiritual guides
- Meeting soul groups
- Choosing your body
- Your life's purpose
- The soul-brain connection
- Visiting the "library" of your life
- Visiting the Council
- Choosing your body for your next life

DOLORES CANNON

Another hypnotherapist whose work focuses on the Interlife is Dolores Cannon. We've seen that Newton uses trance to guide his clients through a past life into the Interlife on a fairly specific path, but Cannon is much more adventurous. She refers to trance in her descriptions of her work, but whereas Newton's clients are only passively aware of the outside environment during his regressions, Cannon is an active participant.

As revealed in her book *Between Death and Life*, where she provides transcripts of regressions she has conducted, Cannon simply guides the client into the trance state, and then chats with them until they have a past life or Interlife experience on their own.

Her method is extremely conversational. Due to her own self-described voracious curiosity, she asks numerous and varied questions in order to glean as much information as possible from the session. Her clients generously oblige.

When they have specific questions they want answered—such as one client who wanted healing for an ailment on the physical plane, and so set out to find some kind of healing center in the spirit realm—she provides a much more focused guidance.

But in cases where no specific outcome is needed, Cannon induces the trance state and begins to ask questions until the client reveals something informative about his or her surroundings. Once such details emerge, Cannon follows the client's lead with her subsequent questions.

The session transcripts in *Between Death and Life* echo the work of Michael Newton. Like him, Cannon found that her regular clients reported consistent information on the Interlife, even though their past-life stories were vastly different.

JOEL WHITTON

Joel Whitton is a psychiatrist who specializes in "re-experiencing therapy"[5] to help clients resolve mental or physical complaints. Author of *Between Two Lives*, Whitton uses a methodology that is, again, similar but different from Newton's and Cannon's.

He treats hypnosis the same way you would use the title menu on a DVD. Pressing the menu button dials up a list of possible destinations on the disc, often called chapters. In our metaphor, the DVD chapters are like the individual past lives.

The client hones in on the life he wants to explore, and Whitton "selects" that life the way you would a specific scene on the DVD. It's as if he is rewinding time to transport the client to the beginning of that past life.

Whitton guides the person through the events of that life, to the death, and then through the death process. In Whitton's recording of these sessions, this stage of the regression can be difficult and painful, but re-experiencing death not only heals any recurring trauma that may be influencing the client's current life, it also processes the client into the Interlife.

One client said, "I'm being flooded with a euphoria that is bigger than I have ever experienced. These feelings are being accompanied by total awareness and understanding of the person I really am, my motives to be, and my place in the universe."[6]

Another said, "I floated into comprehensive golden light. I felt comfortable and warm ... no fear and no solitude ... The golden light surrounded me ... I saw flashes and pastel-like rainbow colors, and I heard hundreds of voices sing simple but nice magical melodies."[7]

Clients also report meeting with a Council of Judgment that manifests as spiritual masters. These judges are benevolent and wish to help people gain understanding.

Notice how the words and phrases echo the terminology and ideas from Newton's and Cannon's research: euphoria, awareness, understanding, motives, place in the universe, golden light, flashes/colors, magical melodies. Despite the variance in regression methods, client experiences of the Interlife share several significant similarities.

ROGER WOOLGER

Whereas Newton, Cannon, and Whitton employ deep hypnosis to explore past lives and the Interlife, Roger Woolger claims hypnosis is unnecessary. Woolger is another authority in past-life therapy whose methods offer a unique synthesis of Jungian active imagination, Gestalt, psychodrama, Reichian body awareness, spiritual psychology, and Shamanic healing.

With these tools, like the regression facilitators we've already discussed, he enables the client to journey through both the past and the Interlife to heal existing and past traumas. He believes wounds can be encoded into the psyche during traumas from past lives. Woolger helps people remember and heal these disturbances, but his process is different.

Woolger calls his technique Deep Memory Process. It is similar to what I know as Somatic Regression. The goal of Deep Memory Process or any form of regression is always the same—spiritual healing.

Woolger says, "I always start from what their present situation is and what they've come to therapy for. I don't do past-life regression for people who are just curious about their past lives."[8] Like the other researchers, he is interested in helping clients resolve issues like marriage, finances, or relationships that they recognize in the current life.

Instead of going straight back to the beginning of the past life, Woolger starts with the present. "After focusing on the issue," he says, "I would regress them back to somewhere in this life where the issue came up, and I would look for clues as they were talking and reliving the experience."[9]

Stage fright is a common example. To deal with this or any fear, Woolger has a client recall a recent incidence of the fear in details as vivid as possible. He enacts how a client might describe this process: "Well, I'm very nervous, my palms are sweating, they're all looking at me, they're expecting me to do something and I'm not sure I'm going to get it right."[10]

Woolger has the client follow the resulting feelings a little further back to an earlier instance. Often this is an event from childhood that is thought to be the original form of the current problem, but usually the situation is more complex. So Woolger presses on, urging the client even further back. Scenarios arise like this one from the stage fright example:

> Suddenly, [the client will] say, "I'm in this cobbled street and my hands are tied behind my back, they're all looking at me!" We've changed it from the current anxiety situation to an anxiety situation that's been lost or buried. [11]

So instead of jumping directly back to the beginning of a past life, like jumping to the beginning of a DVD, Woolger rewinds little by little until the defining moment is revealed.

MY OWN RESEARCH

The process I personally use includes pieces of everyone's work! I use whatever it takes to get the client where they need to go. But then, I add in a whole separate piece so that the client can re-integrate the learned understanding into their current lifetime using the wisdom and insight they have gained.

No matter how the journey is facilitated, there seems to be a process, a route map of the journey through the Interlife with specific stopping-off points. Not everyone stops at every point, but generally speaking, the journeys we facilitate in our clinic follow this map:

- Departure of the soul from a past-life experience
- Soul Permission to take the journey to the Interlife
- Protection for the journey
- A sense of floating or being pulled upward— sometimes through galaxies, sometimes through colors
- A greeting by a light being—one, two or three, who may, or may not be the primary spirit guide
- Passing through an entryway—gates or a doorway
- Meeting with the soul circle
- Visit and stay at the library or laboratory
- Holiday or healing place for rejuvenation
- Council of elders or ascended beings
- Understanding of choice of next lifetime
- Understanding of the purpose of next lifetime
- Place to choose the body to come in with

to complete life purpose
- Trial check of the body including brain circuitry to harmonize with soul energy
- Re-entry into the current life with the knowledge gained
- A follow-up session or two to integrate the information into the current life

Before the journey, I ask the client to list a couple of important people in their current life and to write down some questions we can ask along the way. Nine times out of ten, there is at least one person the client recognizes in the Interlife, and often the questions are answered one way or another before we formally ask them.

Client questions most often include:

- What is the purpose of my current life?
- How can I best get along with my partner / children / parent / family?
- Who am I really?
- Will I meet my soul mate?
- What agreements do I need to work out in this lifetime?
- Why is it difficult for me to be happy?
- Why was my sibling not born?
- Why am I always ill?
- What is blocking my growth in this lifetime?
- Am I meant to always be alone?

Once I started regularly facilitating Interlife journeys, as more and more clients took the journey, and the journey turned out to be the same or similar in structure, I became an absolute believer. What else could explain this phenomenon, particularly as some of the clients didn't know about the

Interlife before coming to the clinic, and certainly hadn't done any reading on it? Often we use these journeys as an extension of a Past Life Regression therapeutic session, so the client's original intent in seeking help is not necessarily spiritual in nature. As the client isn't necessarily expecting this spiritually focused information to surface, the results can't have been "projected"!

Let me take you on a guided journey through the experience and show a little of how some people manifest their particular impressions at each stop along the way. I've included excerpts from regression transcripts I personally have conducted. This will show you how universal and transcendent the journey is for every person who takes it.

1. *Departure of the soul from an earthly or planetary body*

Whether the life is on earth or another planet—whatever causes the end of that life—all healing is given, along with forgiveness of self and others, and the soul rises out of the body to say goodbye. If there are any feelings of remorse, sadness, anger, or guilt, they are left behind in the body in that lifetime and released from the soul/mind through forgiveness and understanding.

Testimonials
- "I can forgive him now—it no longer matters."
- "It feels good to leave that place; even though I had a good time there, it doesn't feel like home."
- "I understand now why she did that; she didn't know what else to do, so I can forgive her."

2. *A sense of floating or being pulled upward*

Sometimes through galaxies, sometimes through colors, there is a feeling of floating, of being gently guided through a series of colors, and coming into a welcoming white light. If the client is moving through galaxies, often they see worlds upon worlds of galaxies unfolding within each other. This is often very moving in its beauty and power. At this point, the client is no longer communicating through the ego or conscious mind, but directly through the super-conscious / soul mind. The client often weeps with a deep joy and sense of "coming home."

Testimonials

- "I felt as if I was being vacuumed up, but it's peaceful. I have nothing to do—just move."
- "I'm floating in something that feels like a red envelope."
- "There's a strong pulling sensation at the back of my head that goes through to my third eye."
- "There seems to be a floodlight lifting me up and carrying me up through the galaxies, one upon the other ... so many galaxies."
- "I'm floating up. There's a strong smell of a flower garden."
- "I seem to be floating through a tunnel, a long tunnel with light all around me. I'm moving into an indigo cloud. My guide is there, reaching down for me and pulling me up. He says, 'Welcome home. You did good, now let's go home.'"

Regardless of the circumstances, client experiences of floating or being pulled up are distinct and profound. Unmistakably, the welcoming vibration that greets each person is calming and comforting in such an overwhelming moment.

3. *A greeting by a light being*

One, two, or three beings of light greet the soul returning home. These beings may take on the demeanor of Buddha, Jesus, or a loved grand-parent, but most often they are some form of swirling light with an aura color. They may or may not be a primary spirit guide, but in all cases, they welcome the client telepathically, either with words or touch.

Occasionally an additional guide will join the primary guide, and this guide may take the guise of the lesson it has come to teach, such as an angel of mercy or a warrior guide. And when that happens, the language and cadence of the speech changes, sometimes drastically.

Sometimes guides even introduce themselves by name. Among the guide names my clients have received are Deo, Noa, Red Feather, Lea, John, and Jarray.

Testimonials

- "He tells me I may call him Ashair."
- "I feel I'm being surrounded by the deepest most profound love—it's as though I'm being wrapped in his color and he's talking directly to my ear. I'm being welcomed home."
- "There is a being with me, and I sense it rather than see it, but if I could see it, it would be about seven or eight feet tall, very tall." (We have found that when the beings

do have bodies, most of the time they are tall and slim.)

- "This guy is greeting me. He's green and wearing a white frock, and he has a white beard. He's sending me feelings and thoughts of love."
- "He seems to be an elderly male being wearing white ... clouds all around him, he is part of the cloud. His name is Ashairazee; he says, 'The life you lived last was quite difficult at the end, but still you did well.'"
- "Your friends are waiting to greet you home; your cloak [earthly body] has gone."
- "My guide is Tibius, and he greets me and envelops me with his love: 'You have done well. I am proud of you.'"
- "My guide has a laughing vibration. It feels joyful being there with him."
- "He tells me that our guides take on a human form so we can recognize them and feel comfortable."
- "It's a light form ... just a wispy orb of light, but the feeling is so peaceful and beautiful."

The purpose of the guide at this stage seems to be to ease the transition into the Interlife.

4. Passing through an entryway

After being welcomed by the light being, most people are taken to an entryway of some sort—the actual entry into their "soul home space" where they will begin the soul healing, learning, the recharging and re-connecting with their peers. As they journey past the entryway and the stops along the way, they often discover their own soul name, soul color, and soul identity that travel with them through many lifetimes.

- "There are buildings everywhere ... made of marble and they keep changing color, rainbow colors, lush green everywhere."
- "Millions and millions of lights ... It's awesome."
- "He says I need healing before I meet my soul group. We go to a place of healing, a circle with something in the middle, like a type of light, pulsing. There's a garden in this healing circle. I'm resting here."
- "He takes me to the place of my soul's birth— a red city—it floats—every being connected to everything in time, all part of each other—we are like scientists. There are other cities like this with other groups [that have] varying roles to play."
- "My guide is telling me I need to rest. He will take me to a place of rest before meeting my soul group. I can't see it, but it feels different ... peace, quiet ... until I'm ready to move."
- "I'm being led into a beautiful garden with a pool and a fountain."
- "I'm being taken to this sort of structure, like a bridge, except it's all light."
- "It's like I'm entering a city of light. All the buildings are translucent. There are buildings for different purposes, all designed by energy beings—schools, a healing place, classrooms, a council building—that is made of purple energy."
- "There is some music playing. It is energetically connected to my soul vibration, and it's healing and balancing me so that I can join my soul circle and be in harmony with them."

Notice the similarities among the testimonials—
the lights, the healing places, the buildings.

5. Meeting with the soul circle

This first meeting often brings tears of joy and
gasps of recognition as the client encounters
people from the current lifetime. Sometimes
clients meet their grandparents, but often it's children or best friends.

Testimonials

- "I go into a chamber where the walls are
  shifting, drifting light of a purple violet color,
  some emerald green, some gold. It's very
  beautiful."
- "Eighteen in a cluster, a cluster of bobbing
  lights. Some are brighter and more advanced
  than the others; it's our job to help them
  move up and join us."
- "There's about 60 people waiting for me. I
  feel love and excitement; they're sending me
  thoughts of happiness [and] love without
  judgment. We have all experienced different
  lives, so we are at different levels of development."
- "My soul friends are there, waiting for me."
- "They are dancing and laughing, welcoming
  me home. They all seem to be wearing wispy
  brown cloaks."
- "They're calling out a welcome ... they are
  calling me Limune—that's my name here.
  They are congratulating me and telling me
  that it was noble of me to spontaneously
  incarnate out of compassion for the parents."
- "There are 24 beings there. The leader John is
  my oldest son ... my grandmother's sister is
  there ... we are all at the same advancement

level. There are other beings in the circle—an elf, a monk—to remind me of my true self. They are reminding me that my earth experience isn't permanent."

- "It feels so familiar. It's a round room with benches, a laughing vibration, [and] 12 to 15 beings there with names to describe their vibrations: Nashot. Krega. Noa."
- "My guide is telling me I have to move on—I've outgrown this group. I need to move to another. I am to become a Master teacher—I have to be with people who understand me and sense the quality of learning I need from this new primary group."
- "I'm violet in color. I am to grow into this understanding. The lesson I am to learn with the group is one of trust."
- "I feel so at home here. This is a place I've been missing for so long ... I feel so sad that I have to leave."

Again, notice the similarities among the reports. The color violet is prominent, as are the sense of lights and the feeling that the beings encountered are "soul friends." Notice how many people discuss the feeling that they are incarnated to learn certain lessons.

6. *Visit and stay at the library or laboratory*
The library or laboratory is the place where souls discover the specific lessons they are meant to learn.

Testimonials
- "As I enter this library place, I'm greeted by a tall being dressed in white. He moves in golden light. His energy is very gentle. He's a

teacher. I'm scared to look in the book he hands me. I ask, 'Can we do it later?' Response: 'You have to do it sometime to know who you are.'" (The client discovers that in a past life he shot his wife and child to death.)

- "I'm being guided into what looks like a laboratory. There are different beakers on tables everywhere, each one containing a different energy frequency. I'm here to learn how to manipulate and understand energies. First I have to heal my own energy. It's a sort of alchemy. My job is group-healing energy—that's what I have to learn."

- "We're going to the library because I need to learn. I need to learn to love my gay energy. If I love myself, I will be able to love others."

Each client learns the specific purpose or issue they are incarnated to resolve. Notice again that even the terminology these individuals use is the same. They all label this stop as the library or laboratory, completely independently of each other.

7. *Holiday or healing place for rejuvenation*
This seems to be the place where a badly hurt or very tired soul can rest and rejuvenate. Although the soul offers itself up to live a life of learning, it seems that somehow, sometimes, it may get more than it bargained for—the learning comes at a heavy price!

Testimonials
- "I am taken to this round room with light pulsing from the walls; it seems as though the light pulses through the walls ... it is suggested I relax in this room until the

pulses slow and stop and I will then be guided further."

- "My guide tells me this is the place where I can bring my vibration back up to the level I need for the rest of the journey."
- "I am to rest and heal here. It's been a very hard and difficult time for me. I need to recuperate, and this is the place. It seems to be a vortex of colors with a sound like I haven't heard before, voices, but not voices— I am surrounded by color and sound—it feels magnificent."
- "There seems to be a room, with beds, but they're made out of light ... shifting and moving ... I am the only one here ... one of the beds is moving towards me ... and I sit and rest here. I feel I'm being wrapped in love, so peaceful and loving."
- "It's a room filled with water! Amazing. Waterfalls. Pools. Fountains. There are beings of light in this place ... one comes towards me and encourages me to enter the pool ... it feels so cool and refreshing ... at the end of the pool is a fountain and I'm joined by others under the fountain ... everyone is laughing ... the feeling is of pure joy. The water becomes me and I am the water ... and the laughter and the joy."

8. Council of elders or ascended beings
This is a place of introspection, and a place where questions may be asked and answered about current and past lives. The Wise Ones or Elders in this space are not here to judge, but to assist and help with understanding and love.

- "I'm being pulled up and up into a white marble room with a big round table and 35 or 36 beings sitting around the table, wearing crimson robes with gold edges. There's a crescent moon symbol on their robes. They remind me that it's all about being who you really are. Make time for peace and consistency of spirit."

- "We enter a space of blue light, [a] semi-circle. I feel so small and humble, and it is huge. There are large thrones with five beings seated. A light comes from the center being. They say they will be easy on me this time. They remind me my body protects my soul, and this one puts a nice frame around me so that people don't see me as fragile."

- "There's a sense of honor and great respect in this space. They want me to step into the column of light facing me so we can communicate."

- "Seven of them, each one wearing something different, but everyone has light emanating from their head and connecting upwards. There's markings on their head, like patterns on the skin. It gives a golden glow. They are sitting with their eyes closed as if in meditation, but communicating with me telepathically. It is a very humbling presence."

- "It's a group mind, and they all speak as one representing a larger whole—I can't quite understand but know it is so."

- "I see a table with seven beings like men. They are wearing deep purple robes. One in the center has an eagle pendant to represent the pairing of vision and sight."

- "This is the council of all of my lifetimes; each one comes from a different city. Red City counselor is the moderator. They look different by choice. They tell me I have five more lifetimes on this planet before I return to the Red City."
- "The communication is telepathic, and I'm tuned into the frequency of love as I enter this space. The message I receive is about feeling deeply. My heart needs to feel as deep as my thoughts, and use the body I'm currently living in, in a more tender way, in a way that touches other human beings."
- "There are four light beings in front of me, and a fifth in the middle is a much higher vibration, wearing either a necklace or a high belt, with a symbol of energy—I feel in my body the pulsing from that symbol."
- "There are four light beings, and they morph into one, then into four."
- "Guys in beige-white robes—all sitting. Even though they don't have bodies, they seem to be sitting."
- "There seems to be [beings] on a large screen looking at me. They are going to show me what has been done well and what should be done better."
- "Marble floors, huge open space. I'm pulled into the door; at the door is a being with a golden staff with a green crystal on the top, in a gold outfit. Inside, three people at the table in silver robes [with] white long hair [are] sitting behind a massive structure. It's a domed room open to the sky. They say [that] if I wish, they could wear more ornamentation; whatever my soul needs they will create."

- "They are smiling. I can feel the vibrations, and they welcome me back—and remind me of the last time I was here."
- "The council room is built like a courtroom. Twelve of them [are] there. They look like wizards! ... dressed in white and gray with large infinity crosses on their chest. They tell me to listen, as I'm continuously being taught, but I don't listen to them."

Once again, the consistencies between cases is astounding. They even use the same language to discuss the council. Many of the council members are "decorated" with symbols, markings, or ornamentation of some kind. Robes are common, as is the sense that the purpose of the meeting is to instruct. Communication is telepathic.

9. *Lessons from the Council*
On this stop in the journey, people are personally addressed by the council. In previous stops, they learn the nature of their life purpose. Here, the council speaks to people directly, giving instructions, "advice," even admonitions, when necessary.

Testimonials
- "You did not ask for our help—you should have. We are here for you. Your journey this time is to learn to give and receive love."
- "You ARE happy; noticing makes you happy—we perceive it as something else."
- "You are capable of so much more. You must push yourself."
- "Don't run from fear. Use it for growth."
- "There is always a fork in the road. Follow other than the ego. Don't be tempted by [the] superficial."

- "It doesn't have to be done in one lifetime. Learning compassion and forgiveness can take a while."
- "Learn and practice stillness."
- "Lighten up with your mother in your current lifetime. She's a challenge [laughing] that was necessary for you."
- "Remember the strength and joy your soul group brings."
- "Enjoy joy!"
- "Let go of the sense of urgency. It doesn't all have to be done on earth—it can also be done from here."
- "Stop judging yourself so harshly."
- "Accept love more easily."
- "Relax in the life you are living and enjoy it. It's only temporary."
- "Your body is the tool you are using to live life. Keep it in good shape."
- "Lighten up with your husband in this lifetime; let him have his own journey."
- "Your resistance causes you sorrow. You are resisting the understanding power of your soul. Your commission is to find the ways of will and love in trust."

10. *Understanding of choice of next lifetime*
Just as Interlife regression can reveal a soul's goals in the current lifetime, it can also reveal the reasons for a soul's choice of future lifetimes.

Testimonials
- "You are to learn patience."
- "To experience and understand joy."
- "To nurture—you will learn how to nurture."
- "Forgiveness is the purpose of this next journey."

- "It is time to lead others, to make change in the world. Choose your body wisely."
- "To stand alone, and not need the energy or presence of another at all times."

A soul has to choose a life that will provide the right circumstances for these kinds of lessons to come through.

11. Understanding of the purpose of next lifetime
Even though souls are meant to learn lessons from each lifetime, this does not mean that your soul's trip to earth is "all about you." You don't just come here to take what the universe offers. You also have to give. Each of us has a life purpose—things we are meant to *contribute* while we're here.

Testimonials
- "Work out how thoughts affect the body and create things which don't exist."
- "I need to connect the grid for new babies coming into the earth planet. We can't have a planet of light if babies are born in pain. It takes too long for the soul to recover, and I have to bring the compassion into bringing in new babies."
- "To learn to use everything I have been given; to go out and look at things differently, according to the way people are living their lives ... not to look for pleasure all the time but for understanding. NOW I understand."

Souls are not here to passively learn. We have to be active in our own process.

12. Choosing the specific body to inhabit for completing life purpose

After a soul discovers the lessons it is meant to learn in its lifetime, it has to find the appropriate life circumstances that will allow it to learn those lessons. Souls do this by "shopping" for a body to inhabit. The process is literally like browsing through a catalog. Souls are shown two or three, sometimes as many as ten bodies to choose from. As they are shown the bodies, they also learn broad facts about the life they would have in each body. In some cases, the soul "tries them on" and takes a trial run. In other cases, they know immediately which body will or will not service the purpose of the future life.

Testimonials

- "There are large angled tablets. The images just come up on the tablets, and it's like watching a video of what could happen."
- "It's like a huge wheel with lots of people being shown to me; I want to understand through a woman's life."
- "It's a dark room. There's another group there making their life choice also ... it's a large room with a blue light. There's a machine with different panels. As it turns, you see different bodies and different lifetimes. There's hundreds there ... then three come forward. I have three choices: a black man with a strong body, but the mind isn't at the level I want. Second choice is a woman, smart mind but the body not right—it will break down when she's young. The third choice is the one I take; it's more balanced for my needs. I go inside to make sure ... it's a healthy body, resilient and

capable. The mind is capable for what it needs to do."

- "There are panels like huge computer screens—I know there are workers there to help me, but I can't see them. These panels are in a semi-circle around me. I see and feel what is on the panels. One panel shows me a middle-class white male in Philadelphia—No ... I want babies! The second panel is a poor woman with lots of children. I would have a good sense of really experiencing—but I don't need to experience suffering to know it. Third panel is a little girl who dies in an accident quite young. Fourth is female, easy life. I could have this if I want it. Five—mother interested in natural childbirth and feeding and lots of children—in Canada, and that's a good country."
- "That body is too frail to do the work."
- "I have to experience unconditional love, as a mother, so I need a woman's body that is strong enough to birth."
- "My self-image and self-worth can't handle extremes right now. I need an average body, but I want one that is and can be active."
- "I chose a female body but would have preferred a regular male body, but I've used that one before."
- "I have a choice of three bodies: male, brown skin, homosexual. Wealthy, blond, blue eyes, female, but her family isn't supportive. Male nomad in the desert. It's a hard life but he will find comfort at the end. I'm choosing the brown-skin male because I have love and support right at the beginning of life, and I want that."

The detail that is most striking is the screens or panels that display the body choices being presented. Here again, the similarities are staggering.

13. Trial check of the body, including brain circuitry, to harmonize with soul energy

Once a soul chooses a body, it runs a "systems check" to discover what vibration it needs in order to accomplish its goals. In addition to checking out the brain circuitry, the person also decides at this time how much spiritual energy they will bring with them into the next life. If it's 60 percent, then that means they leave 40 percent behind to draw on at times of psychic need.

Testimonials

- "I am told to remember that this is only temporary."
- "I have no time for this; my soul is pushing me to come in—you have work to do—GO!"
- "This brain seems to be a bit gummed-up. It's going to take work to sort it out."
- "I'm excited but frustrated. It's going to take this brain time to remember important things, but my goal is to be open and be accepting. I understand this is just a stepping stone."
- "This brain is curious, which fits my soul's needs this time."

Conclusion

I think it's apparent, based on the evidence gleaned from actual regressions, that the Interlife journey is profound. People come away from it with a great sense of inner peace. It's powerful and intense, but also calming and restful. The journey is compassionate and deeply loving, but also instructive and purposeful.

Most significantly, it is universal. Reported experiences are almost eerie in their uncoached similarities. This phenomenon would be amazing enough among clients of one particular hypnotherapist. But as we learned through the research of Newton, Cannon, Whitton, and Woolger, who all use varying methods for guiding the journey, the experiences are the same no matter what.

The knowledge that such a place as the Interlife exists can be frightening in its mystery, but is ultimately comforting. The Interlife journey teaches us there is a purpose for everything. Knowing there is a cosmic order—even if you don't know what it is—is sometimes all you need.

CHAPTER 8

Using the Wisdom Learned

Introducing your Self to your new Self

> They say that time changes things,
> but you actually have to change them yourself.
> ~Andy Warhol

Now What?

So you've done an Interlife regression. You've returned to your normal life, giddy with your new awareness. You've had some revelations. You may have cracked the code to personal mysteries that have haunted you for years. You've had contact with the spirit world, and you have come away from it feeling cleansed, rejuvenated, and blessed. These kinds of feelings are impossible to ignore.

When we move our client into the "Interlife," which we call "between lives" but in reality, it is always there, we can facilitate extraordinary therapeutic interventions which often make radical changes within the client. Letting go of anger, or toxic memories, or the fear to live life to the fullest.

One of the biggest challenges and potential drawbacks of making positive personal changes is weaving those changes smoothly into the fabric of everyday life. It's not always easy to live out the new insights gained during a major spiritual experience. You may have no idea where to even begin changing your own life. Or, you may find that taking the initial steps to institute the changes is the easy part, but getting those changes to stick can be much more difficult.

Either way, you are dealing with significant upheaval. If we build on the premise that most people view change as a difficult and frightening path into the unknown, we know we have lots of work to do.

Plunging headfirst into the unknown of change requires faith—and a plan. This chapter will offer you a plan on how to integrate your new knowledge smoothly into your life. All you have to do is bring the faith!

Introducing the New Self

When people experience sudden positive change, a couple of things can happen. One is that because you are happy about the change, you want everyone around you to be the same and do the same. You may become very eager to share your lessons with everyone you know and everyone you meet.

The people around you can respond to this in one of two ways. They will either buy in and be supportive, trying to understand, accept, and even

> Learn wisdom from the ways of a seedling. A seedling which is never hardened off through stressful situations will never become a strong productive plant.
> ~Stephen Sigmund

learn from this new person that is you—or they will feel resentful and try to diminish the benefits. They may even make aggressive attempts to belittle the efforts and their benefits by making fun or using insults, or they may simply and flatly ignore any attempts you make to discuss the changes.

This kind of dynamic causes all sorts of problems. You may feel like an outsider, unable to relate to the people closest to you. Or you may feel hurt that others are so quick to dismiss what feels so important and life changing to you.

People may be completely annoyed with this New Self. They might feel like you're on a spiritual High Horse, or that you've turned self-righteous. You may seemingly be coming across as judgmental and Above It All. This can rub the people close to you the wrong way.

One way of avoiding this is to just sit with the knowledge for a while. Absorb the new energies you have created for yourself. Then do the plan, as outlined in this chapter, and slowly start making the changes. The folks you care about will notice the changes, and may well learn from your doing, not your talking about doing.

Clearly, integrating the positive personal changes gleaned from an Interlife awakening is a delicate process. If you are to take the learnings and infor-mation from the Interlife into your current life, you need to have the understanding and tools to integrate this new knowledge. You need to be secure within your new is-ness.

This security helps you feel more comfortable; it also helps you integrate new wisdom in such a way as not to cause discomfort to those around you. Remember, it's not uncommon for friends and loved ones to resent change. So, it is important that you have the tools to integrate the changes seamlessly.

The role of your facilitator or regression therapist is to enable you to slowly absorb the new into the old and let go of any outdated or non-useful ideas, patterns, people, or processes.

You do this through the Absorption Process, which we use in the clinic with many of our Interlife or Life Between Lives clients.

The Absorption Process

The Absorption Process is designed to help you smoothly integrate your Interlife journey into your regular life. You'll be able to identify and clarify the lessons learned, the changes that are happening, how they might affect your life and the people around you, and how to deal with those effects.

> The personal life deeply lived always expands into truths beyond itself.
> ~Anais Nin

The process as I use it breaks down into three steps that can be accomplished in three parts, with homework in between. Your Interlife facilitator may have a similar process through which to guide you. If not, you can use our easy-to-follow protocols on your own.

Step One: The New and the Old

To start, you need to make two lists.

LIST 1:   All of the thoughts, feelings, understandings, people, and wisdom you gained from the Interlife journey that you wish to take with you into your powerfully rich future.

The list breaks down into three sections:

- ✔ The people and places I want with me in my future
- ✔ The thoughts and understandings that will carry me into my future
- ✔ The actions, habits, and processes that will enable me to move into my future.

The list should come from what you learned during your Interlife journey

LIST 2:   All the people, places, thoughts, understandings, actions, habits, and processes of your current life that can get in the way of your growth in this lifetime.

You may find that people or patterns you held dear in your life before your journey no longer fit the new self you have embraced—people who rain on your parade, or who are Negative Nellies, or who are intentionally or unintentionally discouraging, unsupportive, or insulting. You may choose to leave these people behind as you move forward. Or you may choose to try to find ways to integrate the new you into life with this person or people so that you don't totally lose them, but rather learn to manage and lessen their impact on you.

Either way, making a list of these people or habits or patterns before the issues arise will help you be prepared for it and be better able to handle it.

Homework One:

Write a journal entry based around the idea of "My New Self." Answer the following questions and any others that come up that you want to explore:

- Who I am today? Who am I into the future?

- What are some of the most noticeable positive changes I feel happening in my life because of my New Self?

- How do I feel about these changes?

- What obstacles do I anticipate I might encounter as I'm trying to accommodate the changes?

- How do I sense those around me feel about the changes?

- How will I present my New Self to the world to allow those in my world to buy in and support my change?

Step Two: The Plan

In this session, you'll be using the previous home-work and refining the description of your New Self. You need practical ways to integrate the changes taking place. Designing a plan of action will help you move forward with new awareness and new perspective.

Look back at the changes you wrote about in the previous session, as well as the obstacles you antic-ipated.

Use the following exercise to identify specific things you can do in your everyday life that will help introduce the changes and help the people in your inner circle accept them.

The top three things I want to change in my life are:

1. _____
2. _____
3. _____

The three things I will do differently every day in my family life are:

1. _____
2. _____
3. _____

The three things I will do differently every day in my work life are:

1. _____
2. _____
3. _____

The three things I will do differently every day in my personal life are:

1. _____
2. _____
3. _____

My first four steps to achieve this new action plan are:

1. _____

    I will achieve this step by this time: _____

2. _____

    I will achieve this step by this time: _____

3. _____

    I will achieve this step by this time: _____

4. _____

    I will achieve this step by this time: _____

Homework Two:

Start the "sell" to the outside world by taking at least one step of the action plan. You might like to write a journal entry about your experiences while enacting the plan, answering the following questions:

- What step of my action plan did I choose to take first? Why did I choose this as my first step?

- What difficulties, if any, did I encounter in taking this step? How well did I handle it?

- What was the most gratifying part of this step? What validation did I receive—from another person, from myself, from the universe?

Step Three: The Future

The purpose of this session is to give you the ability to carry out the remaining steps of the action plan, and then maintain that focus into the future.

Update and re-assess how far you have come with your plan. Using the results of *Homework Two,* review the area of change you chose to approach first, the action taken, the difficulties faced, and the validations experienced.

You may have fears or concerns about completing the action plan. You can let go of those fears by identifying the difficulties you may face in the subsequent steps of your plan. You might even benefit from answering question number 2 from the exercise in *Homework Two*—What difficulties did I encounter, and how did I handle them?—for each step of the plan. But instead of answering the question *after* completing the step, answer the question *before* completing the step, sort of as a preliminary prep tool.

Just this little bit of further preparation can make a profound difference in the experience of instituting change. It offers many advantages, not the least of which is the confidence that comes from feeling ready for whatever might occur.

Another advantage of having a well thought out plan for action is that you will be more capable of repairing any damage that may come into your relationships. When a difficulty arises, you won't be caught off guard and freeze. You'll know what to do to heal the situation.

This is the time to use self-hypnosis or meditation to confirm the changes in your subconscious mind. I have made a self-hypnosis CD for people to use who aren't sure about the practice of self-hypnosis, so you could work your plan with that, and once you've learned how, that ability will stay with you for the rest of your life. A gift to yourself!

Also, learning self-hypnosis will enable you to re-charge your own batteries any time you find your energy and focus are waning.

Conclusion

The moment one definitely commits oneself, all sorts of things begin to happen that would never otherwise have occurred.
~Goethe

The Interlife journey reveals profound, life-altering lessons. You return from these journeys filled with joy and wonder and enthusiasm over the new revelations. You'll probably be eager to integrate the revelations into your life, but change like this is never easy. It's a delicate process. It's easy to make mistakes that can alienate you from people you care about. If this happens, the temptation to abandon the changes can be strong.

It would be a big shame to waste the deep and reaching experience of the Interlife simply because you don't have the tools to bridge the gap between the spiritual world and the concrete. This chapter is your tool. Use it well and with joy, because it is the start of a new you! And you can never un-know that!

CHAPTER 9

Choosing Your Regression Therapist

True teaching is not an accumulation of knowledge; it is an awaking of consciousness which goes through successive stages.
~Proverb on Ancient Egyptian Temple

You are about to embark on a soul journey, and as such, it should be taken with respect and humility. For a facilitator, it is an honor to be invited to journey with your soul, and your experience with your chosen facilitator should reflect that.

Be as clear as you can with your regression therapist about the purpose of your journey. List some of the important people in your life, how they have impacted you, both positively and negatively, and have some questions written down that he or she can ask for you along the way.

Because integrity and trust are so important in any spiritual or regression work—or indeed any therapeutic work at all—I have four key suggestions to give that will help you choose an appropriate regression therapist to ensure your Past Life, or

Interlife journey is a profound and satisfying experience for you.

1. Do your research. Check out the regression facilitator's training, level of experience. Is it full time or a weekends-only practice for them? How long have they been working with clients? Go onto the Web site of the training school your intended facilitator learned from—and make sure they're listed. If not, ask why. (Check the Addenda for some reputable schools that teach Regression Therapies.)

2. Talk to them at their office, either in person, or on the phone. Ask questions. Ask about the process. Ask if they record the session, and how. Ask if they have a Code of Ethics they follow—if so, who wrote it. (See Codes of Ethics in the Addenda.)

3. How do you "feel" about the facilitator? Do you trust them? Do you feel comfortable with them? Do they listen to you, or are they too busy talking about themselves and their expertise?

4. Ask about fees and timing. For a Past Life Regression session you need at least two hours, for an Interlife session, at least three hours. The fees should reflect this. If someone you speak to is a lot cheaper than another facilitator, beware—they might not be as experienced, or as well trained.

Once you have chosen:

- Allow time to relax after the session. Don't plan a party or dinner with friends to discuss it. You won't want to ... for a while anyway! It takes time to absorb all the information you have received. You will be emotionally touched—and you will probably want your space.

Once in the session:

- It is your journey; you are in charge. Which means, it is up to you to allow the facilitator to take you into deep trance so that your superconscious won't be interrupted by your conscious mind. You don't need the ego on this journey!

- Allow your soul to speak, to show you how magnificent you are, and how you impact the lives of others.

Choose your facilitator wisely, and then relax and let them guide you through this intense and moving process. I promise you, your life will be forever changed!

CHAPTER 10

Some Common Questions and Answers

*Do you really want to look back on your life
and see how wonderful it could have been
had you not been afraid to live it?*
~Caroline Myss

- Is there a better time of day to have a Life Between Lives session?
You're probably better at the start of the day rather than at the end of a day. At the end of the day you may be tired, and because you will be so relaxed and comfortable, you might be inclined to fall asleep.

- How long is the average session?
Generally speaking, you need to allow a minimum of three hours. Sometimes a little less, sometimes more, but the average is three hours.

- Will I remember everything in the session?
Absolutely! Not only will you remember it, it is recorded for you so you will be able to re-visit the journey.

- Are there any negative side effects after a session?
The only side effects might be that you feel awed by the journey itself, and it might totally occupy your mind

*for an hour or two after the session. This is why we
suggest you not plan any social event after the session,
but rather allow yourself some quiet time for an hour
or two.*

• Can someone come with me into the session?
*Preferably not because there is always a part of you that
knows you're being watched and listened to. The goal
is for you to be completely relaxed and for the journey
to be private and confidential. Should you wish to share
it with friends or family afterwards while listening to
the recording, it's your right and privilege to do so, but
I strongly recommend that the spiritual space being
created by you and your facilitator be just for the two
of you.*

• How can I be sure I'm getting an appropriately
trained facilitator?
*First, check and see how and where they were trained.
See how long they have been in business as a hypno-
tist. Finally, and most importantly, spend some time
talking to them, even on the phone, to make sure you
feel comfortable and trusting with them.*

• Will I meet my soul mate on this journey?
*Nothing can be guaranteed. This is a soul journey and
you are taken where you need to go at this time.
However, most people meet with their soul circle, and
sometimes within that circle is their soul mate.*

ENDNOTES

Chapter 1: What *Is* the Interlife?

1 Joel L. Whitton, M.D., Ph.D. & Joe Fisher, *Life Between Life: Scientific explorations into the void separating one incarnation from the next.* (N.Y.: Warner Books, 1986), 26.

2 Winafred Blake Lucas, Ph.D. *Regression Therapy: A Handbook for Professionals Volume 2.* (Deep Forest Press 1993), 198.

3 Whitton, op. cit., p. 15.

4 Ibid, p. 74.

5 Leonard Jacobson, *Journey into Now: Clear guidance on the path of spiritual awakening.* (La Selva Beach, CA: Conscious Living Publications, 2007), 211.

Chapter 2: What Is This State We Call Death?

1 Robert A.F. Thurman, trans., *The Tibetan Book of the Dead.* (NY: Bantam Books, 1994), 23.

2 Ibid, p. 23-24.

3 Dolores Cannon, *Between Death & Life: Conversations with a spirit.* (Huntsville, AR: Ozark Mountain Publishers, 1995), 199.

4 David Staume, *The Beginner's Guide for the Recently Deceased: A comprehensive travel guide to the only inevitable destination.* (St. Paul, MN: Llewellyn Publications, 2004), 67/68.

5 Ibid, p. 2.

6 Migene González-Wippler, *What Happens After Death: Scientific & personal evidence for survival.* (St. Paul, MN: Llewellyn Publications, 1997), 72.

7 Dolores Cannon, *Between Death & Life: Conversations with a spirit.* (Huntsville, AR: Ozark Mountain Publishers, 1995), 190.

8 Ibid, p. 236-37.

9 Ian Lawton, *The Book of the Soul: Rational Spirituality for the Twenty-first Century.* (Rational Spirituality Press, December 1, 2004), extract from chapter 6, "Choosing Lives During the Interlife."

10 Palden Jenkins, "Psychic Abortions" (1999), http://www.palden.co.uk/palden/p4-childbirth.html

Chapter 3: Reincarnation and Life After Death

1 Rabbi Elie Kaplan Spitz. *Does the Soul Survive? A Jewish journey to belief in afterlife, past lives & living with purpose.* (Woodstock, VT: Jewish Lights Publishing, 2000), 144.

2 Ormond McGill, *Grieve No More, Beloved: The book of Delight.* (Wales, UK: Crown House Publishing Limited, 2003), 36.

3 Francesca Fremantle and Chögyam Trungpa, trans. *The Tibetan Book of the Dead.* (Boston, MA: Shambhala Publications Inc., 1975), 3.

Chapter 4: The Role of Karma

1   Masaru Emoto and David A. Thayne *The Hidden Messages in Water* Atria (September 20, 2005).

2   From *Anatomy of Spirit* by Caroline Myss, Ph.D., copyright © 1996 by Caroline Myss. Used by permission of Harmony Books, a division of Random House, Inc.

3   Ibid.

4   Robert A.F. Thurman, trans. *The Tibetan Book of the Dead*. (NY: Bantam Books, 1994), 28.

5   Richard McLean, *Zen Fables for Today*. (New York: Avon Books, 1998).

6   "Karma." http://www.buddhism.kalachakranet.org/karma.html. 8 November 2007.

7   Ibid.

Chapter 5: Your Soul and Soul Mate

1   www.rachelkeene.co.uk/soulgroups.html

2   Ibid.

3   David Bennett. ww.dharma-talks.com/soul_group.htm

4   From *Anatomy of Spirit* by Caroline Myss, Ph.D., copyright © 1996 by Caroline Myss. Used by permission of Harmony Books, a division of Random House, Inc.

5   www.stanford.edu/group/hopes/basics/braintut/ab5.html

6   Neale Donald Walsch. *The Little Soul and the Sun: A Children's Parable Adapted from Conversations With God*. Hampton Roads Pub. Co. (April 1, 1998).

Chapter 7: Mapping the Journey

1   "What is Trance?" http://www.spiritualregression.org/trance.html

2   Ibid.

3   "Life Between Lives." www.pascashealth.com/Pascas-Health-Life-between-Life.pdf

4   Ibid.

5   "Stichting Spirituele Ontwikkeling." www.spiritualiteit.com

6   Ibid.

7   Ibid.

8   "Kindred Spirit, Past Lives." www.kindredspirit.co.uk/ARTICLES/4843_past_lives.asp

9   Ibid.

10 Ibid.

11 Ibid.

ADDENDA

A. How to Rescind a Soul Contract

If ending a soul contract interests you, here's how to do it. First, you need to take yourself into a hypnosis trance, or meditation, to connect with your higher self.

* Ask your guides if it is appropriate for you to rescind your soul mate vows at this time. If you have not yet resolved all of the past karma between you and your partner, you will not be permitted to rescind the vow. You can also use a pendulum if it is easier for you to dowse for a yes or no answer.

* Once you have agreement to go ahead, light a white candle and cup your hands, palms down, over the flame, asking the energy from the white light to clear your energy field and create a place of balance from where you can make your request. Ask your guides and teachers to join you to assist you in rescinding your vows made with (NAME OF PARTNER). Bear in mind that you can only release someone through love. Anger doesn't really work as a release since it creates a magnet that bonds energy rather than dissolving it.

* Imagine bringing the white light from the candle through to your body, and ask that Creator Love, Light, and Truth be present throughout your physical, spiritual, mental, and emotional being as you make your request.

* Mentally envision the partner you are releasing and bring your hands over your heart, conjuring the intense and heightened feeling of the love you initially felt when you entered the relationship, prior to the conflict. Sometimes, envisioning your partner as a child makes it easier to feel this love energy.

✳   Hold the love energy in your hands and move your hands over your head, palms up. Release the energy into the atmosphere.

✳   (SAY:) "I acknowledge the love I have felt for (NAME) in the past. I retain that feeling of love while releasing the emotional chord that continues to bind me to (NAME)." After stating these words, envision the severing of a silver cord that connects your heart to your previous partner's heart. Bring your end of the silver cord into your own heart, much like retrieving a fishing line by reeling it in. Feel the release of your energy from that of your partner's energy.

✳   Complete the ritual by saying, "So let it be" after extinguishing the candle flame.

B. Soul Circle Meditation Script For Self-Recording

If you don't have access to a regression facilitator, you can still use self-hypnosis or meditation as a way of tuning in to the spiritual realm. The following script is an example of such a journey. If you don't have a professional regression facilitator, you have two additional choices. One is to record yourself reading this script and play it back for yourself as you relax. It may take a few tries until you receive the same benefit as you would if you did the journey with a therapist or facilitator. You could also have a trusted friend read it for you if you'd rather not have the experience alone.

"Do what you need to do to make yourself comfortable. Close your eyes and notice your breath ... as it flows in and out. Feel the coolness as it flows in ... and the warmth as it flows out. Allow yourself to feel more and more relaxed with each out breath ... flowing in and flowing out ... flowing in and flowing out ... the coolness of the inflow ... and the warm outflow.

Re-arrange your arms and legs as comfortably as you can. Focus on your breath ... the warm outflow of each breath takes you deeper ... and deeper ... and deeper ... gently breathing, never ending, the cycle of breath ... flowing easily and gently.

Take a moment now and go inside yourself to find the source of your breath ... take a moment and honor that part of you ... the part that allows and monitors your breath, allowing your brain to function with oxygen and your heart to continue its life-affirming rhythm.

Go inside to find your pulse, the beat of your heart, and notice how it has slowed down ... how it has relaxed along with your mind ... as you follow your breath ... now take a moment ... and thank and bless that part of you ... your heart ... that allows you to live and love and take part in the world at this time.

Now take a deep breath … let it out … and go still deeper into a place of deep relaxation, where you are aware but completely relaxed. As you imagine being in the most wonderful place … a safe place, a place where you feel most relaxed … a place where you feel the most good … imagine how it looks … is it inside or outside?

And as you picture or think about what it is like … notice how your body is becoming more and more relaxed with every out breath … the warmth of the out breath takes you deeper … and deeper into relaxation … as you see yourself now … sense yourself now … in this wonderful place where you feel the most good … the most relaxed … the most safe …

Maybe it's a beach … maybe it's a comfortable chair in your home … maybe it's the dock at the cottage … whatever it is … it is your safe place … just see it in your mind … and feel the relaxation it brings in your body … you may even notice some sounds associated with this place … birds singing, or water trickling … or the sound of leaves rustling in the breeze … or there may just be a very peaceful silence … and each breath takes you deeper … and deeper into relaxation … every out breath takes you deeper … and deeper…

As you imagine yourself relaxing in your safe, wonderful place … maybe feeling the warmth of the sun on your skin … if you're on a beach … or the comforting feeling of being in familiar surroundings … if you're in a favorite chair at home … whatever is right for you … is right for you … and it allows you to relax so completely … and more completely than you have relaxed in a long … long time … with every breath going deeper and deeper into relaxation …

And as you continue relaxing now … your mind is opening to the awareness of a powerful healing spirit within you … during this time … this session … your subconscious mind will only accept suggestions that are totally safe and in line with the highest good of your entire being ... Any suggestions you accept, will function in the ideal time frame and in the safest and most comfortable ways. If in the future, any of the suggestions become outdated, or fail to serve your highest good ... they will automatically dissipate and disappear from your mind.

Letting go ... now ... even more, with every breath, noticing that every third out breath doubles your relaxation ... it happens ... easily, automatically, without any thought on your part ... easily .... effortlessly ...

Imagine a flight of stairs, a beautiful golden staircase leading you into the deepest state of relaxation. As I count down from 1 to 10, allow yourself to drift down these stairs, lightly and gently with each breath, drifting down ... deeper ... 1 ... 2 ... deeper and deeper ... 3 ... 4 ... moving down into a deep state of relaxation, where nothing bothers you, nothing disturbs you, going down ... 5 ... 6 ... letting go ... the deeper you go, the better you feel ... 7 ... 8 ... all the way down now ... 9 ... and 10 ... deeper and deeper.

If you so choose, you may ask that your higher power be present to guide and protect you during this program ... and throughout the mind-body balancing.

As your body relaxes, you may begin to feel pleasantly blurry and distant ... As you relax more ... and more ... you may allow yourself to connect into the helpful flow of the universe ... the ebb and flow of the water ... the clouds passing by ... and per-haps even the warmth of the sun. That's right ... in this beautiful relaxed state you can connect into the power and beauty of the universe.

In a moment—but not right now—I will ask you to lend me your imagination and go to your favorite place ... see and feel how wonderful it is ... how peaceful and calm ... the more you focus on where you are and the colors and textures, the smell and sounds ... the deeper into relaxation you go.

So now ... for a short while that seems like a long while ... focus on what you can smell in your wonderful space ... breathe in ... gently but deeply now ... the faint fragrance of flowers perhaps ... or the sea ...

And now ... if you listen very carefully, what sounds can you hear? ... Maybe the sound of birds ... or music in the distance ... or even water, trickling and soothing to your ears ...

And look very carefully at what you can see ... or imagine that you can see ... look at the colors ... notice how the light falls on the colors ... notice the textures ... maybe you want to reach out and touch the textures to feel the differences under your fingertips ...

Letting go all of your day-to-day concerns ... just relaxing down ... following your ... breathing ... and notice how smoothly and freely your breath is flowing ... smoothly ... freely ... flowing breath ... bringing oxygen down to your lungs ... smoothly and freely ... your breath flows ...

Now ... as your breath flows easily and smoothly ... allow your mind to access your deep, healing wisdom ...

Now imagine, if you will, in this beautiful, wonderful safe place, a magic line that allows you to journey back through time and space. This line is like a moving highway, and when you choose to step onto it, it will carry you back ... back ... through time and space, very quickly through months and years of your current life, into the womb of your mother ... that dark warm place where you can feel the heartbeat. Rest there for a moment, and feel the heartbeat of your mother, surrounding you, healing you, connecting you to all there is where you are right now ... feeling safe and protected.

And as you move, feeling pulled or floating safely ... floating and moving ... you may see a light ... a bright white light, or a cluster of lights ... waiting to greet you on your journey. Take your time and move toward the light. It may be your primary guide. Just notice what you sense or feel or see.

How does this welcome being manifest itself for you? Is it someone you recognize? Does it have the shape of what we call a human being? Is it male or female, or does it exists for you as light or energy, waiting with love to greet you?

Notice how you are greeted. Are you surrounded by the energy of love, or does your guide move toward you, arms outstretched to welcome you? Just relax, note and enjoy the pleasure of this greeting ... Notice the color of your guide's aura ... and ask, if it is appropriate for you, for your guide to give you their name.

Now ask your guide to tell you your soul color ... and listen with your heart for the answer.

Ask, if it is appropriate for you, to know your soul name ...that name which travels with you since time began ... ask now for your soul name ... and listen with your heart.

When you are ready, your guide will take you to meet the souls in your soul circle ... those souls with whom you have made agreements and contracts to play out different lives with you at certain times, different lives to fulfill an agreed-to contract and karmic agreements—even those that caused you pain, as these souls lived that life with you and for you, so that you could experience the lessons you needed to learn at that time, and maybe still do.

These souls who help you on your journey are your true soul mates, soul mates who come in and out of your lifetimes, over eons of time, to teach, to learn, to share, and to love. Your soul mates.

So journey now on this exciting journey to meet your soul mates, your true partners in the soul journey.

Notice where your guide is taking you ... and how you get there. Are you floating? Are you being pulled or do you suddenly appear somewhere with your soul circle waiting for you?

Arrive now at the place of your soul circle ... notice how you arrive and what you see there ... I will take the time to give you the space to experience all you need to experience in this journey.

Notice how your soul group shows itself to you. Do they take on human form, or are they lights moving around singly, in pairs, or in clusters? Just notice what you perceive ... maybe you see them and maybe you don't, but however you receive this information, take note of it ... now ... are they in a circle, in a line in front of you? Or all bunched up?

As you come toward them, are you in the center ... or do you join together as one large cluster of brightness? Notice how it feels to be surrounded by those you travel with through time and space, through many lifetimes ... notice how you are received, how they greet you.

How many of them can you see?

As you get used to being with them and feeling your place with them ... notice which one comes forward first to greet you. Is it a male or female energy? Is this person in your life today in any form? Have you shared other lifetimes with this person? What is this soul's immortal name?

What role does this soul have in your life today—or in your soul growth? Does it offer balance? Or show you kindness and generosity of spirit? Does it bring you experience of hardship so you may learn? Just be aware of your link and relationship with this soul.

Now look around at the other souls in your group. Who are the ones you have most often incarnated with in your past lives? Who is in your life today? What role do they play in your life today?

Notice what feelings and thoughts you are receiving from your group.

Ask them to give you some messages that you may bring back with you to enhance your current life.

Thank them and bid them farewell for a short while, which may seem like a long while. They remind you that you are—in truth—together all of the time. Separation doesn't exist.

Notice that certain phrases emerge from your heart that express what you wish most deeply for yourself, not just for today, but in an enduring way. Phrases that are big enough and general enough that you can ultimately wish them for all of your current life, for your loved ones ... for all beings everywhere ... You hear the murmuring ...

"May I live in safety. May I be happy. May I be healthy. May I live with ease."

You gently repeat these phrases over and over again, as you journey back through the galaxy, back through the vibration of what we know as time. All people, all animals, all creatures, all those in existence, near and far, known to us and unknown to us. All beings on the earth, in the air, in the water. Those being born, those dying.

You feel the energy of this aspiration extending infinitely in front of you, to either side, behind you, above and below. As the heart extends in a boundless way, leaving no one out, may all beings live in safety, be happy, be healthy, live with ease.

Slowly and easily, you are being guided back to what we call the present time. Slowly changing your vibration, coming back now … to the present time … on this planet earth, at this present day.

As you enter the here and now … in a moment, I will count from 10 to 1 and you will return to full awareness, feeling grounded, alert and ready for the life you live today.

10, 9, 8, 7… move your fingers and feet … 6, 5, 4 … shrug your shoulders … 3, 2, 1 …

Fully awake now.

May *you* live in safety. Be happy, be healthy, live with ease."

C. Energy Healing and Clearing Script

(You may choose to have someone read this to you, or record it for regular use. It is a wonderful script to use before any energy work.)

"By Divine Decree, in the name of God Presence, through the law of grace, love, forgiveness, karma and divinity, I now break and dissolve all vows, agreements I may have made across time, space and all dimensions in relation to closing my mind, heart and soul to any new experiences and transmitting cynicism, disbelief, mistrust or negativity about new ways of being, change, transformation and the Power and Presence of Spirit and Love within all beings.

By Divine Decree, in the name of God Presence, through the law of grace, love, forgiveness, karma and divinity, I now break and dissolve all vows, agreements I may have made across time, space and all dimensions in relation to denying my God Presence and my trust in the wholeness of my being, the prosperity, infinite power of love and light, held by my being.

By Divine Decree, in the name of my God Presence, through the law of grace, love, forgiveness, karma and divinity, I now break and dissolve all vows, agreements I may have made across time, space and all dimensions in relation to holding, storing, repressing onto any feeling, thought form or unresolved memory around the breaking down in the flow of my trust, faith and love and my harmony, alignment and balance and the sense of interconnectedness of my soul with all other beings. So be it."

CODE OF CONDUCT FOR
ETHICAL CLIENT-CENTERED PAST LIFE RESEARCH
AND REGRESSION JOURNEYS

Ethical Past Life Regression and Life Between Lives Journeys are the experience of the client and in no way reflect the thoughts, feelings or channelings of the facilitator or practitioner.

1. The client experiences the journey in a kind, safe and trusting environment.
2. Soul Permission is asked before embarking on the journey.
3. Protection and help is asked before embarking on the journey.
4. Upon completion of the journey, forgiveness, compassion and love are given to the person in that lifetime.
5. Upon completion of the journey, forgiveness, compassion and love are given to those who shared that journey with the client.
6. Joy and wisdom from that life are explored and brought forward into the current day.
7. The journey is closed off leaving all pain and discomfort behind the veil.
8. The client is returned in fullness to the current time and place and encouraged to document and bring wisdom and learning into their current lifetime.

As a fully trained client-centered Past Life and Life Between Lives facilitator, I promise and commit to the above code of ethics and practice.

Name _____ Date _____

Issued by The Ontario Hypnosis Centre Clinic and School, Toronto, Ontario, Canada

E. Code of Ethics II

THE NEWTON INSTITUTE CODE OF ETHICS FOR LIFE BETWEEN LIVES PRACTITIONERS

In the sacred quest to provide a meaningful LBL experience, practitioners use all of their skills, training, and experience to reconnect their clients to the loving wisdom of the spirit world. In recognition of the intuitive nature of LBL facilitation, practitioners remain open to spiritual guidance when conducting sessions.

Practitioners provide their clients with a safe and caring professional environment. The profound trust inherent in the client-practitioner relationship is respected, and therefore each LBL session is conducted with courtesy, sensitivity, and patience.

Informed consent is always obtained from clients after imparting clearly and honestly the range of experiences that may be realized in an LBL session. Financial policies are declared in advance, and fee arrangements are resolved before beginning a session.

Individual advertising and promotional campaigns are truthful, and realistic statements are made regarding client outcomes. Personal qualifications are communicated clearly; factual information on relevant certifications and professional affiliations is fully disclosed to clients and prospective clients upon request.

Complete confidentiality is honored and maintained for each client, as well as for the spiritual beings who may come forth in an LBL session. All client-practitioner communications are confidential. Client permission must be granted when recording a session and when sharing or publishing session material. Records are preserved in a secure environment to ensure privacy.

The purity of LBL therapy as a stand-alone discipline is protected. When offering non-LBL services during the course of LBL therapy, practitioners advise clients that such services are beyond the explicit endorsement of The Newton Institute.

In order to expand the understanding and practice of LBL therapy, practitioners may share session records with The Newton Institute's research department after appropriate permissions have been obtained. Practitioners stay informed of new advances in the field by participating in LBL eGroups, attending Institute trainings, conducting research, and pursuing other relevant educational opportunities whenever possible.

Practitioners honor collegial relationships by cooperating with all of The Newton Institute's officials and members. Practitioners speak respectfully of colleagues, and will not solicit another practitioner's clients.

As ambassadors of The Newton Institute, practitioners work to illuminate public awareness regarding LBL therapy. Practitioners conduct themselves in such a manner as to uphold the integrity of LBL therapy and The Newton Institute above any individual.

BIBLIOGRAPHY & ADDITIONAL READING

There is a noble and exciting heritage and ongoing research of writing, recording and researching the Interlife, Life Between Lives, or Bardo. Here are some of the better-known names of the community worth researching.

Authors:

Robert Buckman – *Human Wildlife: The Life that Lives on Us.* The Johns Hopkins University Press (February 14, 2003).

Dolores Cannon – *Between Death and Life: Conversations with a spirit.* Huntsville, AR: Ozark Mountain Publishers, 1995.

_____ *Jesus and the Essenes.* AR: Ozark Mountain Publishers; New Ed edition (December 1, 1999).

_____ *Legacy from the Stars.* Gateway Books (GIMA) (May 10, 1999).

Georgina Cannon – *Return: The Healing Power Of Your Past Life Regression.* OHC Publishing (September 30, 2004).

The Dalai Lama, Jeffrey Hopkins and Tenzin Gyatso – *The Meaning of Life.* Wisdom Publications; Revised edition (November 1, 2000).

Hazel Denning – Author, Lecturer

Francesca Fremantle – *The Tibetan Book of the Dead.* Trans. Francesca Fremantle and Chögyam Trungpa. Boston, MA: Shambhala Publications Inc., 1975.

Elisabeth Hallett – *Soul Trek: Meeting our children on the way to Birth.* Light Hearts Publishing (September 1995).

Jeffrey Iverson – *In Search Of The Dead: A Scientific Investigation Of Evidence For Life After Death.* BCA (1993); and BBC TV series.

Susan Kelleher – *Spirit Dogs: Life Between Lives.* Owl of Athene Press (June 1, 2005).

Winafred Blake Lucas, Ph.D. *Regression Therapy: A Handbook for Professionals Volume 2.* Deep Forest Press, 1993.

Gates McKibbin – *The Life of the Soul: The Path of Spirit in Your Lifetimes.* McKibbin Publishing, Inc. (October 15, 1999).

Michael Newton – *Journey of Souls: Case Studies of Life Between Lives.* Llewellyn Publications; 1st ed edition (September 1, 2002).

_____ *Life Between Lives: Hypnotherapy for Spiritual Regression.* Llewellyn Publications (May 1, 2004).

A.P. Sinnett – *Life Between Lives.* Kessinger Publishing, LLC (December 8, 2005).

Dr. Ian Stevenson – (Director of the Division of Perceptual Studies at the University of Virginia) *Where Reincarnation and Biology Intersect.* Praeger Paperback (May 30, 1997).

Dr. Joel Whitton – *Life between Life: Scientific explorations into the void separating one incarnation from the next.* Joel L. Whitton, M.D., Ph.D. & Joe Fisher. N.Y.: Warner Books, 1986.

Migene Gonzáles Wippler – *What Happens After Death: Scientific & personal evidence for survival.* St. Paul, MN: Llewellyn Publications, 1997.

Roger J. Woolger – *Healing Your Past Lives.* Sounds True Inc., U.S.; Har/Com edition, 2004.

Additional Reading:

David Bennett – Dharma-Talks.com

Leonard Jacobson – *Journey into Now: Clear guidance on the path of spiritual awakening.* La Selva Beach, CA: Conscious Living Publications, 2007.

Ian Lawton – *The Book of the Soul: Rational Spirituality for the Twenty-first Century.* Rational Spirituality Press (December 1, 2004). www.awakening-spirits.net/book.htm (Phone: +31-75-6230043).

Ormond McGill – *Grieve No More, Beloved: The book of Delight.* Wales, UK: Crown House Publishing Limited, 2003.

Caroline Myss – *Anatomy of the Spirit: The Seven Stages of Power and Healing.* Harmony Books (Random House, Inc.) 1996.

Rabbi Elie Kaplan Spitz – *Does the Soul Survive? A Jewish journey to belief in afterlife, past lives & living with purpose.* Woodstock, VT: Jewish Lights Publishing, 2000.

David Staume – *The Beginner's Guide for the Recently Deceased: A comprehensive travel guide to the only inevitable destination.* St. Paul, MN: Llewellyn Publications, 2004.

Robert A.F. Thurman – Trans. *The Tibetan Book of the Dead.* NY: Bantam Books, 1994.

ORGANIZATIONS & SCHOOLS

Organizations: American Society of Psychical Research www.aspr.com

IARRT (International Assoc. of Research and Regression Therapies)
http://www.iartt.org/contactus.htm

Michael Newton Group, The Newton Institute
http://www.spiritualregression.org/code_of_ethics_e.htm

PEAR
http://www.princeton.edu/~pear/

Princeton Engineering Anomalies Research
Society for Psychical Research
http://anomalyinfo.com

Schools: Ontario Hypnosis Centre School and Clinic
1-866-497-7469
www.ohcclinicandschool.com

The Newton Institute
http://www.spiritualregression.org/

International Association for Regression Research
and Therapies
www.iarrt.org

Dolores Cannon
http://www.ozarkmt.com/cannon.htm

WEB SITES

ARE
Association for Research & Enlightenment
The Edgar Cayce Foundation
www.are-cayce.com

Childen's Past Lives Research Center
www.childpastlives.org

IARRT
International Association for
Regression Research & Therapies Inc.
www.iarrt.org

IBRT
International Board for Regression Therapies
www.ibrt.org

INDEX

Learn Hypnosis With Our Hypnosis Training Courses

and become a Past Life Regression Facilitator.
The first step on your path is to

Take our Hypnosis Training Course and become a certified NGH Hypnotist!

Course Accredited by the largest international body of hypnotherapists, the National Guild of Hypnotists

Graduates may apply for membership to the
International Hypnotherapy Federation and The International Medical and Dental Hypnotherapy Association

You will be able to use the powerful tool of clinical hypnosis to enable yourself, or your clients in smoking cessation, weight control, stress management, self-esteem, pain management and goal setting techniques.

Upon graduation you'll also be qualified to run group hypnosis sessions for smoking cessation, weight loss, relaxation and goal setting.

Levels One and Two of this program are given at one time, so that you may practice immediately upon graduation. The program features small groups, lively and interactive learning, combined with a warm, helpful environment for your success.

- This pragmatic intensive curriculum is designed to allow the practitioner to practice the classical approach to hypnosis.

- You will learn the appropriate and approved applications for hypnosis, client assessment, trance techniques and client self-hypnosis techniques.

- Course includes two 100-page workbooks for ongoing learning, all video and audio tapes, induction and testing sheets, chevreuils pendulum and other materials for successful client work.

- On graduation you will receive a diploma and be accredited by the National Guild of Hypnotists

- Graduates have an automatic one-year membership in the National Guild of Hypnotists, which entitles you to:
    - Referrals through computer listings
    - Hypno-Gram quarterly newsletter
    - Journal of Hypnotism quarterly magazine
    - Video rental library for members
    - Annual Conference
    - Book, tape, and video discounts
    - Hotel/motel and auto rental discounts in the U.S.
    - Continuing education programs.

Contact: www.ontariohypnosiscentre.com for more information.

The Past Life Regression Facilitator Course

is based on the work of Henry Bolduc,
Dr Milton Erickson and Edgar Cayce

Because clients who are hypnotized sometimes "slip into" past or former lives when working to change something in their current life, the professional hypnotherapist needs to understand how to work in this field in an effective, healing and ethical way. This is a soul journey process which includes forgiveness, healing and wisdom. We also cover life between lives and the journey and decisions made before birth, Karma and choice.

- A three-day, intense, pragmatic, interactive and profound training program
- Past Lives, between lives, the decision and journey to this life
- Bringing forward the wisdom and understanding the relationships around the current life
- Researching for mental, physical or emotional pain
- Unique intuition expansion sessions
- Group and one-on-one practice sessions

A spiritual and profound three days that will make a difference to your life!

For further information contact us at
www.ontariohypnosiscentre.com.

The Life Between Lives—
Your Interlife Workshop

This workshop will demonstrate and teach you how to access soul memories through a trance-induced "superconscious" state of awareness that brings a deep sense of love, compassion and an understanding of our life purpose.

Based on the work of Michael Newton and Dolores Cannon, this workshop is unique in that it also teaches how to bring the learnings into the client's current life experience and issues.

Registration Requirements:
Minimum of 100 hours of formal hypnosis education certification and ongoing clinical practice; Past Life Regression training certification and clinical practice.

Because we believe the best way to learn is to experience the process yourself, during the training and practice you will personally experience an enhanced understanding of why you chose to come into your current life, why you have had to face specific challenges during this lifetime, and what other soul needs are being met and fulfilled in this current lifetime.

At the close of this course you will have a deeper commitment to live your "soul's contract" or life's purpose. Once you pass your exam and graduate, you will be able to bring this profound work into your practice and your community.

For further information contact us at:

www.ontariohypnosiscentre.com

Send Us Your Stories!

Do you have an interesting Past Life Regression or Interlife stories that affected you dramatically and could fit into one of these categories?

- A physical health change
- A major life change
- How your journey helped you beat the odds
- or change your Karma
- or led you to your current life partner
- or introduced you to your soul mate

If your story is appropriate for one of our future books and we would like to include it, we'll give you full name credit – if you wish. If your story fits into our book outline we will contact you to receive your approval and find out more! It could be fun!

Send your stories to:

> georgina_cannon@returntopastlife.com
> *or*
> Dr. Georgina Cannon,
> Director, Ontario Hypnosis Centre,
> 94 Cumberland Street, #310,
> Toronto. Ont. M5R 1A3
> Canada

Also ... Now that you've read this book, maybe you'd like to see more books like this. Take a few minutes and check out our Web site at:

www.ontariohypnosiscentre.com

and let me know if there's something there you would like to learn more about – in the same easy-to-read and absorbing style as this book. I'm currently working on my next two books and am always interested in hearing from readers about what interests them.

If you send me your thoughts about another book, I promise to respond personally to you. You can write to me about your new book idea at georgina_cannon@returntopastlife.com

Order Your Copy Today!

RETURN

Past Life Regression and You

To receive your copy of

RETURN: *Past Life Regression and You*

simply complete the form below and mail to:
**Ontario Hypnosis Centre, 94 Cumberland Street, Suite 310,
Toronto ON M5R 1A3 Canada**

Please send me

_____ copies at $24.00 each

Price includes applicable taxes, shipping and handling charges.

TOTAL : _____ copies x $24.00 = _____

PLEASE PRINT CLEARLY

My name is _____

Number and Street _____

Apt number _____

City _____

State or Province _____

Postal Code or Zip Code _____

Country _____

Phone _____

email (print) _____

Enclosed is my cheque ☐   **OR**   Bill to my credit card ☐

Cheque ☐   Credit card ☐   Visa ☐   Master Card ☐

Number _____

Expiry Date _____

Name on the card _____

Signature _____

Order Your FREE
Past Life Regression CD

If you can't find your way to a Past Life Regression Facilitator, you might want to experience the journey through the power of your CD player!

   As our gift to you, we will send you the CD "Past Life Memories" – absolutely free. Retail Price is usually $22.50. Because we want you to understand our passion and commitment to this process, all we ask is that you pay $5.00 for shipping and handling.

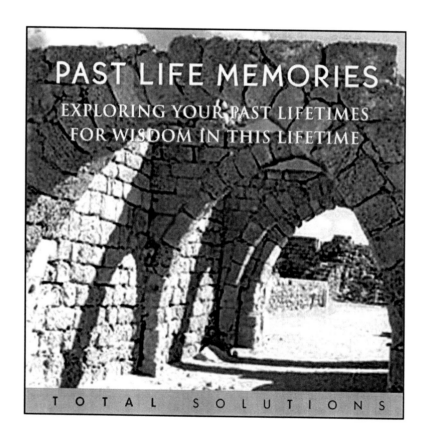

To receive your FREE CD simply complete the form below
and mail to: **Ontario Hypnosis Centre, 94 Cumberland Street,
Suite 310, Toronto ON M5R 1A3 Canada**

Just carefully remove this page from the book, fill in your name and
address, add your credit card number or cheque for $5.00 (sorry, no
cash through the mail) and you will receive your free disk within
10–14 days.

PLEASE PRINT CLEARLY

My name is _____

Number and Street _____

Apt number _____

City _____

State or Province _____

Postal Code or Zip Code _____

Country _____

Phone _____

email (print) _____

I am enclosing the $5.00 shipping cost for my free disk by:

Cheque ❑   Credit card ❑   Visa ❑   Master Card ❑

Number _____

Expiry Date _____

Name on the card _____

Signature _____

I purchased my book:

Name and city of bookstore _____

       through the Internet   ❑

       through the publisher   ❑

       through conventions/training/courses   ❑

CD List

ALL CD'S ARE $22.50 PLUS APPLICABLE TAXES AND SHIPPING. FOR BULK ORDERS, PLEASE CONTACT: info@ontariohypnosiscentre.com

1. **HEALING THE BODY** — This healing CD program will enable you to prepare your body for surgery or heal chronic or acute conditions by communicating with your body at the very deepest, cellular level.

2. **PAST LIFE MEMORIES** — Explore past life-times, safely and ethically, with this self-hypnosis CD.

3. **MOVE FORWARD WITH CONFIDENCE** — Find the confidence and creativity to move forward in your life, and make changes NOW.

4. **HYPERTENSION RELEASE** — A self-hypnosis journey to lifelong health and balance, enabling the reduction of hypertension once and for all.

5. **STOP SNORING** — Sleep deeply and quietly every night with this self-hypnosis program.

6. **LETTING GO OF STRESS** — An empowering, decompressing self-hypnosis program for anyone who needs to relax and allow the world to be a stress-free place.

7. **CREATING ABUNDANCE** — Create success, joy and love in your life. Let self-hypnosis help you to manifest the abundance you seek.

8. **STOP SMOKING FOR LIFE** — Take back control and be smoke-free for life with this self-hypnosis program.

9. **YOUR JOURNEY TO THE AKASHIC RECORDS** — Using the power of hypnosis, you can enjoy a spiritual soul journey that will enable you to find your soul purpose, your soul name, and maybe even your soul mate.

10. **IMPROVE YOUR SEXUAL PERFORMANCE** — Dream, explore and rediscover the possibilities of your own sensuality and sexuality.

11. **STARTING OVER** — This is an empowering self-hypnosis program that uses two voices for maximum success to access the left and right sides of your brain — both the creative and pragmatic parts — to enable you to move forward.

12. **RELAX AND REJUVENATE** — A renewal of self to refresh and relax your energy. Using the power of hypnosis, learn to bring harmony and balance back into your life.

13. **SLEEP ANYWHERE, ANYTIME** — This gentle self-hypnosis CD teaches you how to ease into sleep wherever and whenever you wish. Awake in the morning feeling refreshed and ready for your day.

14. **CHAKRA BALANCING** — A gentle hypnotic journey to balance and rejuvenate mind, body and spirit. Harmonize and explore your Chakras, their meaning and energies.

15. **ENLIGHTEN UP FOR LASTING WEIGHT LOSS** — This is a step-by-step weight loss program that is designed to increase your self-esteem, build your inner strength, and bring focus to your inner goals and life.

16. **COOLING THE FLASH** — Manage the symptoms of menopause and go about your daily life without hot flashes.

17. **MANAGING IRRITABLE BOWEL SYNDROME** — Learn to use the power of your mind to help alleviate the pain and discomfort.

18. **FORGIVENESS & HEALING THE INNER CHILD** — Forgiveness is an empowering act that allows you to move forward in peace and joy.

19. **PROCRASTINATION GONE** — Understand why you procrastinate and reprogram your subconscious mind to create and accomplish your goals.

20. **RELEASE FEAR OF FLYING** — Using the power of your mind you learn to release the fear and reprogram your thoughts to travel with freedom.

21. **SELF HYPNOSIS** — This is a gift you can give yourself for the rest of your life. Learn to use your subconscious mind to benefit every aspect of your life.

22. **MEETING YOUR SOUL CIRCLE** — Go on the journey to the Interlife and experience a connection with your true self. And maybe meet your soul mate.

23. **DUMP THE JUNK** — Going beyond stuck. Clear out your clutter, get rid of old cobwebs or skeletons in your closet.

24. **PUBLIC SPEAKING WITH EASE** — With regular use of this CD program you will learn how to feel relaxed and confident when presenting in front of any number of people.

25. **EXERCISE FOR YOUR HEALTH** — Visualize your success in achieving your health and wellness goals.

CD Order Form

ITEM	UNIT PRICE	QUANTITY	TOTAL PRICE
1. Healing the Body	$22.50	X _____	= $ _____
2. Past Life Memories	$22.50	X _____	= $ _____
3. Move Forward with Confidence	$22.50	X _____	= $ _____
4. Hypertension Release	$22.50	X _____	= $ _____
5. Stop Snoring	$22.50	X _____	= $ _____
6. Letting Go of Stress	$22.50	X _____	= $ _____
7. Creating Abundance	$22.50	X _____	= $ _____
8. Stop Smoking For Life	$22.50	X _____	= $ _____
9. Your Journey To The Akashic Records	$22.50	X _____	= $ _____
10. Improve Your Sexual Performance	$22.50	X _____	= $ _____
11. Starting Over	$22.50	X _____	= $ _____
12. Relax & Rejuvenate	$22.50	X _____	= $ _____
13. Sleep Anywhere, Anytime	$22.50	X _____	= $ _____
14. Chakra Balancing	$22.50	X _____	= $ _____
15. Enlighten Up For Lasting Weight Loss	$22.50	X _____	= $ _____
16. Cooling the Flash	$22.50	X _____	= $ _____
17. Managing Irritable Bowel Syndrome	$22.50	X _____	= $ _____
18. Forgiveness & Healing the Inner Child	$22.50	X _____	= $ _____
19. Procrastination Gone	$22.50	X _____	= $ _____
20. Release Fear of Flying	$22.50	X _____	= $ _____
21. Self Hypnosis	$22.50	X _____	= $ _____
22. Meeting Your Soul Circle	$22.50	X _____	= $ _____
23. Dump the Junk	$22.50	X _____	= $ _____
24. Public Speaking with Ease	$22.50	X _____	= $ _____
25. Exercise for Your Health	$22.50	X _____	= $ _____

SUBTOTAL = $ _____

IN CANADA ADD 5% GST = $ _____

Bill to my Credit Card VISA ☐ MasterCard ☐

Card # _____

Expiry Date _____

Signature _____

☐ Enclosed is a cheque made payable to:
   Ontario Hypnosis Centre

Subtotal = $ _____

Discount = $ _____

Shipping = $ _____

TOTAL = $ _____

SHIP MY ORDER TO:

Name _____

Address: _____

City, Code _____

Phone: _____

AVAILABLE DISCOUNTS
10–30 CDs = 15% discount
30–50 CDs = 25% discount
50+ CDs = 40% discount

SHIPPING CHARGES

Quantity	CANADA	US
1	$2.50	$3.50
2	$4.00	$5.50
3–5	$6.00	$7.50
6–10	$7.00	$9.50

About the Author

DR. GEORGINA CANNON, a certified master clinical hypnotherapist, is an international award-winning teacher, lecturer and director of a hypnosis clinic and school in Toronto, Canada. For over a decade since its founding, Dr. Cannon has initiated the ethical protocols and procedures for regression now followed by her students and many others in the regression field.

Often called upon by radio, television and print media, Dr. Cannon was involved in a major network television series on past life regression (Past Life Investigation) which is currently being shown on the History and Discovery Channels and around the world. She is also a regular host of the Shirley MacLaine Web site chat room, and a regular contributor on REMFM radio in Spain and Xzone Radio world wide. Dr. Cannon also meets regularly with medical and wellness professionals to enhance their knowledge and awareness of hypnosis and the dynamic healing potential of soul or past life journeys.

Dr. Cannon is on the advisory board of the National Guild of Hypnotists and is their accredited instructor to train hypnosis teachers in Canada.

NOTES

NOTES

NOTES

NOTES